Justice and Troubled
Children Around the World

Justice and Troubled Children Around the World

Volume I

Edited with an Introduction by

V. Lorne Stewart

New York University Press
New York and London

Library of Congress Cataloging in Publication Data
Main entry under title:

Justice and troubled children around the world.

Includes index.
1. Juvenile courts—Addresses, essays, lectures
2. Children—Legal status, laws, etc.—Addresses,
essays, lectures. 3. Juvenile delinquency—Addresses,
essays, lectures. 4. Child welfare—Addresses, essays,
lectures. I. Stewart, V. Lorne.
K5575.Z9J87   345.73'08   79-3154
ISBN 0-8147-7809-7 (v. 1)

Manufactured in the United States of America

THE DECLARATION OF THE RIGHTS OF THE CHILD.
THE UNITED NATIONS

The Right

    to affection, love, and understanding

    to adequate nutrition and medical care

    to free education

    to full opportunity for play and recreation

    to a name and nationality

    to special care, if handicapped

    to be among the first to receive relief in times of disaster

    to learn to be a useful member of society and to develop
       individual abilities

    to be brought up in a spirt of peace and universal
       brotherhood

    to enjoy these rights, regardless of race, colour, sex, relig-
       ion, national, or social origin.

Foreword

The publication of *Justice and Troubled Children Around the World* may be a golden key to the baffling walls still surrounding the problem of delinquency. For many years Dr. Eleanor Glueck and I urged international studies of this basic question. Though varied cultures influence philosophy and practice in the field of child welfare, a synthesis might bring to light the *universals* operative as causal agents in juvenile delinquency and so lead to prevention and, hopefully, "cure" when the damage has been done.

Judge Stewart's long experience with troubled young people at The Family Court of Metropolitan Toronto and his work in juvenile justice with the United Nations makes him the ideal person to bring together the experience of others in dealing with juveniles in many parts of the world. Scattered studies have been made in several countries, but all too often these researches have not been generally known and not applied. This well may be the work which will give to practitioners at many levels workable ideas for the direction of their own endeavors in improving the quality of life for children and their families.

Sheldon Glueck
Roscoe Pound Professor of Law Emeritus

Harvard Law School
Cambridge, Massachusetts
September 12, 1979

Contents

Editor's Introduction

V. Lorne Stewart

The Changing Faces of Juvenile Justice[1] written in response to a growing concern about children in conflict with the law, dealt with existing national remedies in the area of delinquency control in seven countries. The reaction has been such that an obvious need exists for a more comprehensive treatment of the expanded subject of care as well as control of children. *Justice and Troubled Children Around the World* will provide the reader with vital material based upon the career exposure of highly qualified persons to problems, issues, trends and decision making in the closely related areas of child neglect, child abuse and juvenile delinquency. They describe national efforts to become more effective through the co-ordination of health, educational, welfare and legal services. They emphasize the importance of the home, and of the need to relate its positive influence to the whole effort of the community to raise the quality of life of both young and old.

While it is reasonable to assume that crime prevention begins in early childhood much of a nation's concerns about its children lies before and outside its conscious efforts to prevent either delinquency or crime. Its focus is upon providing adequate and appropriate food to sustain life and growth; careful and skilled

---

1. V. Lorne Stewart (ed.), *The Changing Faces of Juvenile Justice* (New York: New York University Press, 1978).

instruction in knowledgable skills and values deemed necessary by the community; and opportunities for the child to develop its potential both as an individual and as a maturing and responsible member of society. In a more complete view of the place of the child in society one need but look at the Declaration of the Rights of the Child enunciated by the United Nations. The natural and unfrustrated growth of children is predicated upon the ability of society to guarantee the satisfying of those basic needs which make these rights a categorical imperative.

When children's rights are ignored and the needs left unfulfilled, aberrant behavior can be expected to appear in a variety of forms. How such conduct is described and cataloged depends upon the tolerance levels and value patterns of the section of society that has the power to take action to remedy the situation. Needless to say, history and current observations show how far from uniform are the social policies in different countries. A delinquent act in one place may be regarded as a maladjustment in another or as a community default in still another.

Thus, when dealing with the subject of children in the real world which surrounds them, there is a danger that we will classify their conduct as right or wrong, good or bad, pre-delinquent or delinquent too quickly. Much should be expected of the community to contain the child within safe parameters: the home, the school, the church, the local helping agencies. However, realism must of necessity prevail and at some point—when danger signs accompany the misconduct of the child—responsible persons must view the behaviour as predictive and demanding special attention. Even at this point the community should proceed with caution in deciding how to act. It is here that the term prevention begins to have meaning. We have crossed the line from early child welfare concerns to an area where a community's fear of negative responses has arisen. In some places the term predelinquency has been adopted to describe this phenomenon. The Gluecks of Harvard University alerted us to the early manifestation and seriousness of such conduct. They saw it as predictive and demanding early preventive action:

When to the tender age of school misbehaviour there is added the early age of first delinquent behaviour (almost half the delinquents were under eight years old at their first delinquencies), it becomes crystal clear that *the signals of persistent delinquency flash their warning before puberty.* This means that the elementary schools are in a strategic position to discover *potential* delinquents before the trends of maladapted behaviour become fixed.[2]

As we study the etiology of delinquency and the history of corrections, we observe that no definitive universal answers have as yet been discovered. Each country pursues its own methods of prevention and cure and this seems as it should be. Some prefer to delay the decision to classify miscreant children as delinquent law breakers by applying a procedure better understood as a form of social justice. In other places there has been a ready use of judicial proceedings as early as the accepted age of criminal responsibility would allow.

The pendulum of juvenile justice has swung in wide arcs in many places during recent years.[3] There is every indication that it will continue its nervous and restless response to changes in social and political philosophy, to public alarm over acts of violence by young people, and to the accelerated application of the skills of educators, behavioral and social scientists, and sociologists to the problems that surround youth. The juvenile court is but one actor in this drama that starts early in the life of a child—perhaps much earlier than we had anticipated—with the plot unfolding in a gradual, relatively uneventful fashion with many youngsters but in a much more explosive and rebellious manner with others. But appearances may be deceiving. The quiet, unresponding youngster, lost or hidden in the womb of

---

2. Sheldon and Eleanor Glueck, *Ventures in Criminology* (London: Tavistock Publications; Cambridge, Mass.: Harvard University Press, 1964), p. 28.

3. Stewart, op. cit., p. 1.

the home or classroom, may be engaged in an inner warfare of distressing proportions. Who can tell where his fear, indecision, and rebellion may take him? When, within the broad expanse of child development, we separate out, perhaps ghettoize, and designate a part of the whole as the property of juvenile justice, is there not a danger that we may be capturing those that should be treated otherwise? Where do we draw the line between the child who needs care and protection and the one who needs to be controlled by extraneous inventions such as the juvenile court? If the community agencies cannot control the uncontrollable, who can? If it falls the lot of the juvenile court to do by authority what schools, agencies, and clinics cannot do by persuasion, what kind of court must it be? How much more than law must the judge know if he or she is to be the leader of a team of corrective experts too frequently dealing with the child "from the other side of the tracks"? Must a type of professional esperanto be invented so they can understand and accept one another? Or is the pendulum swinging in some other direction perhaps toward the imposition of "coercive sanctions appropriate to the seriousness of the offence"?

Justice and Troubled Children Around the World will take the form of a series of books dealing with neglected and delinquent children in a substantial number of countries. It is hoped that the first two volumes will be published in 1980 as a contribution to the literature being encouraged by UNICEF. It is hoped that volumes three and four will be released before the Sixth United Nations Congress of Crime Prevention and Treatment of Offenders. Subsequent volumes will follow. If highly significant developments take place in the field during publication of the series, space will be reserved to update previous national presentations. It is hoped that the series will bring together varying philosophies, policies, points of view, techniques, and practices for serious study. While responsibility for each chapter will be left with its contributor, it must be recognized each speaks with authority based upon long experience. It is not intended that this should be a comparative study. Conclusions reached by the reader will have to be a private matter. *Justice and Troubled Children Around the World* was simply conceived as a partial answer to the question so often asked, "How do others deal with their troubled children"? There are troubled children all over the world and this series is an attempt to get workable answers to that question.

It is appropriate that this series should be introduced by Professor Emeritus Sheldon Glueck of Harvard University who has contributed so greatly to extending the horizons of understanding about delinquent children. My personal indebtedness to him spans many years during which he shared insights, knowledge and friendship. In all probability this international venture would not have taken place without his support.

ACKNOWLEDGEMENTS

The encouragement and assistance of Professor G.O.W. Mueller in conceptualizing the problem of troubled children as it is early associated with crime prevention and in producing this series is greatly appreciated. His knowledge and concern about children finds expression in many ways in these books. It was he who recognized the importance of placing Juvenile Justice on the agenda of the Sixth United Nations Congress on the Prevention of Crime and the Treatment of Offenders.

Thanks is also given to the staff of UNICEF's International Year of the Child Secretariat, especially to Dr. Estefania Aldaba-Lim. John Grun, Edward Marks, and Danica Adjemovitch, for the sharing of vision and compulsion to do more for the world's children while time is still on our side.

His Excellency Mr. H.W. Barton, Ambassador and Permanent Representative of Canada to the United Nations and Mrs. Barton have shown a continuing interest in this effort to share knowledge about children and their problems. Their sensitive understanding of troubled children has been an inspiration.

The co-operation of Sheila Murphrey of Harvard Law School in helping to set the direction of this series is greatly appreciated.

About the Contributors

Professor Stanislav V. Borodin
Director of the Research Institute of the Ministry of the Interior. Moscow.
Member of the United Nations Committee on Crime Prevention and Control.
Participant at the Meeting of Experts on Juvenile Justice held in the Judicial College of the University of Nevada. 1979.

Judge Alyrio Cavalieri
Judge of the Juvenile Court in Rio de Janeiro, Brazil.
Vice President of the International Association of Juvenile and Family Court Magistrates.

Dr. Saied Ewies
Counsellor at the National Center of Social and Criminological Research. Cairo, Egypt.

Dr. Josine Junger-Tas
Special Consultant to the Minister of Justice on matters relating to delinquency. The Hague, Netherlands. Author of many articles and books in the field of family welfare.

Mrs. Akka Kulkarni
Former judge of the Juvenile Court in Bombay, India. A lawyer and social worker. An active member of the International Association of Juvenile and Family Court Magistrates.

Social Judge Erik Munch-Petersen
Ankechef. Chief of Appeals of the National Social Appeal Board. Copenhagen, Denmark.

Dr. David Reifen
Former Chief Judge of the Juvenile Courts in Israel.
Author of *The Juvenile Court in a Changing Society,* and many other publications. Editor-in-Chief of *Society and Welfare.* Lectures at the Center of Criminology, Tel Aviv University.

Professor Jose Arthur Alves de Cruz Rios
Head of the Department of Sociology, Catholic University, Rio de Janeiro, Brazil. Participant at the United Nations Meeting of Experts on Juvenile Justice held in the Judicial College of the University of Nevada in 1979.

H. Veillard-Cybulska.
Mrs. Henryka Veillard-Cybulska is the Deputy Secretary General of the International Association of Juvenile and Family Court Magistrates. She resides in Lausanne, Switzerland. Her publications, including those written in association with her late husband Professor Veillard-Cybulska, cover the law and social work as applied to problems of children and families.

ABOUT THE EDITOR

Judge V. Lorne Stewart (Retired), former Senior Judge of the Provincial Court (Family Division) for the Judicial District of York in Toronto, Canada. He was consultant on Juvenile Justice to The Law Reform Commission of Canada. Expert consultant on Juvenile Justice to the United Nations in New York, Fellow of the Centre of Criminology at the University of Toronto and former Faculty member. He holds graduate degrees in Psychology (University of Toronto) and Sociology (University of Pennsylvania). He is Vice-President of the International Association of Juvenile and Family Court Magistrates. His publications include the following: *The Changing Faces of Juvenile Justice* (ed.) New York University Press, 1978; "Sheldon and Eleanor Glueck of Harvard" in *The International Encyclopedia of the Social Sciences,* Free Press, 1979. *Youth Crime and Juvenile Justice: International Perspectives* with Paul C. Friday (eds.), Praeger Publishers, 1977.

1

Brazil

Alyrio Cavalieri and Jose Arthur Rios

Alyrio Cavalieri, distinguished Brazilian Judge and Vice-President of the International Association of Juvenile and Family Court Magistrates, has joined with Professor Jose Arthur Rios, Head of the Department of Sociology at Catholic University in Rio de Janeiro, to produce an overview of the services provided for children in Brazil. This is a rare statement combining the product of two minds—one sociological, the other legal—both focussed upon the conviction that the best solution to crime is to improve the quality of life in early childhood. They trace the history of child welfare in Brazil, discuss transitional problems and trends, describe new laws applied to children, and analyze Brazil's efforts to co-ordinate governmental and private social services.

Editor

1. BACKGROUND

In order to become even superficially acquainted with the child's predicament in Brazil, one has to look at the wide context of the country's development in the last decades. Recently, the

1

National Foundation for Children's and Youth Welfare (*Fundacao Nacional do Bem Estar do Menor*) or FUNABEM as it is better known, estimated as 14 million the total population of abandoned, deprived, deviant, and delinquent children in the country. These are defined by the Foundation itself as lacking the minimum level of living in order to cope with their five basic needs of health, education, recreation, social security, and—according to the Foundation statute—love and understanding.

Children's problems have been disregarded until recently in Brazilian society because they were imbedded in a wide area of poverty. At least 30 percent of the Brazilian population lacks permanent work and live below minimum salary levels. In 1970, a third of Brazilian families earned a little more than US $10 monthly and two thirds of our economically active population earned less than US $50 monthly.

Brazilian sociologists have identified this stratum in slum areas, in the outskirts of big cities, and in rural areas, and called it marginal or tending to a marginal position. It is usually understood that such a condition is due to very low incomes—lack of participation in the consumer market—as well as to its incapacity to afford the basic services, housing, health, work, and leisure. Such strata of the population are physically present in Brazilian society mostly as migrant, temporary, and unskilled laborers, who have proved unable to make use of and to participate in social and market institutions.

In rural areas, labor is scarce, due to the basic features of our agrarian structure, still firmly anchored in the agro-industrial plantation and the archaic *latifundia*. Both are conducive to the same result—a lack of social stability as represented by permanent employment and continuous family life. Massive migration to the cities follows, stimulated by the concentration of public investments in urban areas and by the official ideology of *desenvolvimentismo* (development for development's sake) consciously or subconsciously oriented by a Marxist ideology of industrialism at all costs. The Brazilian technocrats have dis-

2

regarded agriculture, the improvement of standards of living in rural areas, and all this has led to chaotic urban growth and the resulting lapse of many people in the proletarian status.

In the 1950s, rural migration was absorbed by the new factories subsidized by public money, but in the 1960s migration to the cities increased. Marginalization—a big word to denote a wide process—spread in urban areas and increased slum areas from clusters of a hundred shacks to the size of real slum cities housing 100,000 people. A change in labor legislation introduced in rural society a new type, the vagrant laborer, who sells himself to the highest bidder and does not live in the plantation itself but in rural slums, in the outskirts of small towns or in agricultural areas.

A wide spectrum of social problems was brought up by the new wave of urbanization and by the trend of economic growth at all costs—from mere unemployment to vagrancy, absolute poverty, loss of cultural values, high birth rate, marginal activities such as beggarism, drinking, violence and crime, prostitution and the abandonment of children.

Poverty, absolute poverty, is the root of the mass problem. After a careful survey of FUNABEM's 100,000 files that were collected from 1966 to 1974, the Foundation experts verified that a situation of destitution—total lack of family support or any tutorial protection—was responsible for the seclusion of 10 percent of its inmates.

In a recent study (1974) the World Bank analyzed the condition of poverty in Brazil, and came to rather optimistic conclusions as to the general improvement of the majority, which achieved relative high marks in their income levels. Nevertheless, it acknowledged that the increase of income in certain brackets determined a loss, in absolute terms, in the lower strata.

According to World Bank estimates, almost 7 million families might be considered poor in Brazil. They represented 32 percent from the total of 21 million Brazilian families. The Bank classified as poor those families spending less than two minimum

3

salaries, in money or other exchange, at the time about US $1,300 a year. Estimating in 5 people—the average number of people per family, their *per capita* income would range from zero to US $260 a year, or from zero to US $20 monthly. More than half of those families lived in the northeast, the drought and poverty ridden region, where they represented 61 percent of the total number of families in the area. According to the same study the great majority of families in rural areas might be considered as poor, whereas in the metropolitan regions only 11 percent would be classified as such.

More significant, the study registered a serious unbalance in the numbers of temporary landless laborers *(boias frias)*. They increased about 50 percent between 1960 and 1973. Moreover, it was noticed by the authors of the study that three fourths of the urban poor are more concentrated in cities and small towns than inthe metropolitan areas.

In general, the levels of income of the poor have been underestimated in the past; but, to the contrary, the supposed higher levels of income for the general population due, by the way, to social vertical mobility and the shifting of jobs rather than to upgrading salaries, do not alter the implicit conclusion that real poverty, as such, was not reduced. This can be seen, as a matter of fact, in the high levels of malnutrition, infant and general mortality, a short life expectancy, lack of services, and poor quality of life. All these related to the population included in the lower income brackets, or, for that matter, below two minimum salaries.

In short, although the real income of all groups has presented a substantial growth, the income of people in lower brackets during the seventies has tended to grow less than has the income of those in the other strata, and the economy showed a definite trend to income concentration. The discussion now turns around the question whether the poor have participated less in the country's development or have become marginalized.

This general overview is a necessary introduction to families'

4

predicaments and children's troubles in a country plagued by chronic inflation, where a conception of development based on state centralization and industrialism determined an imbalance between regions (poor, agrarian northeast as against the prosperous, industrial south), and between rural and urban areas as well. Out of this imbalance, migration to the cities and to jobs become to millions of poor rural laborers the only way out.

These data and further research lead to the inescapable conclusion that children's troubles in Brazil arise basically from social structure and not—as foreigners and political radicals sometimes are prone to conclude—from a lack of social agencies or from official indifference.

2. THE LEGAL ANGLE

Till a very recent date, Portuguese medieval law was the precedent for everything prescribed for children and young people. It was a mixture of ancient Germanic, customary, and Roman law. As such, the norms governing children's behavior are included in the Philipine Ordinations—inforced in Colonial Brazil since 1603. It is quite impressive to notice how lenient and understanding these norms were. The law maker, for instance, relied heavily on the judge's evaluation of the offense, instead of prescribing an *a priori* punishment.

"And in such cases [when the offender is 17 to 20 years old] the Judge will consider the offense and its circumstances and the youth's character; and if he will find him with malice and deserving capital punishment, will apply it, even through natural death. But if he assumes that the offender does not deserve it, he can decrease the penalty, according to the quality or simplemindedness of the offender."[1] It also prescribed, in the case of

---

1. *Ordenaçoes,* Luis V, Título CXXXV.

young people less than 17 years old, that the judge would not, in any case, apply capital punishment but would use his judgement to apply a more lenient sentence.[2]

Besides the Ordinations, the law relies on an old concept of childhood, dating back to Roman times. Infancy—*infantia,* when we are not able to speak—was singled out as the time of life where people would not be law conscious and would not be endowed with penal responsibility. However, young people from 12 to 14 would be looked at, from the legal point of view, more as adults than as children. When judges started applying the norm *malitia supplet aetatem,* punishments became more severe and the so-called *pubertati proximi* (12 to 14 years) received sentences very similar to those applied to adults.

In colonial legislation, the first mention of abandoned children is found in a royal decree, dating back to 1693, in which the Governor of Rio de Janeiro was instructed to deliver abandoned or rejected children to the care of the Municipal Chamber, to be fed on that public body's funds. At that time, the decree did not mean much, since the first boarding house for rejected children was only established in 1738.

After independence, Brazil turned away from the archaic Portuguese law and started to elaborate its own legislation. The first criminal code dates back to 1830. It was based on the rules of the Classic School which assumed that moral responsibility should be based on free will. From this assumption it follows that the agent's will is the basic condition for punishment. A criminal act would presuppose *mala fide,* that is, knowledge of good and evil, malice, and intention to commit the offense. These criteria of discerning ability would mark Brazilian penal law about juvenile delinquents during all the nineteenth century and the first decades of the twentieth.

Thus, people younger than 14 were not singled out as criminals. They were considered absolutely immature. As to offenders in higher age brackets, the judge would intern them in the so-

2. Ibid.

called correction houses. The judge was the only one to evaluate their condition, according to his own criteria. However, when in 1864, an infant 5 years old, was brought to court, the Supreme Court decided to exempt children 7 years and younger of any penal responsibility.

The 1890 Penal Code, sanctioned after the Republic, would assume the same philosophy, but, in the case of juveniles between 9 and 14, substituted prison for educational and disciplinary measures. Idealistically, it introduced the internment into "industrial establishments," but, since they were unknown to the country, the young offenders were put in prisons. Judges tried to correct the anomalous situation by having children and juveniles placed in the correction houses, a minor solution. In fact, an executive decree in 1893 determined the internment of vagrants, truants, and trouble makers in these correction houses; and, for the same purpose, equated juveniles, without parents or tutors to the latter's condition.

The first change in the system was made only in 1925 and was due to the enlightened endeavor of a juvenile court judge, Jose Candido de Albuquerque Melo Matos, who fought for a reform in the legislation and, in the best French tradition, for a special code for children and young people. Since 1921, due to his efforts, the principle of discrimination was derrogated by excluding of any process of law people below 14 years and by establishing that offenders, between 14 and 18, should be submitted to a special procedure.

For the first time, the concept of abandonment was legally defined. It considered as abandoned all the children lacking material or moral support and orientation from responsible people, who might represent them in court. It also considered abandoned those associated with bad company, or seen in disreputable places, or subjected to ill treatment.

All this was the result of Melo Matos campaign. In his *Rules* he also introduced, in place of probation, the notion of supervised freedom. He applied it to children in reform school, and created the first juvenile court in Rio, then the Federal Capital.[3]

For the first time children's and youths' rights were the object of a specific law similar to the civil code or the penal code. Brazil was one of the first countries in the world to have such a legislation.

Within the system of the juvenile code, the troubled children were divided into abandoned and delinquent, both under 18 years. According to legal definitions, abandoned children suffer physical deprivation, due to permanent or temporary lack of parental or tutorial care. They are found in places, or, for that matter, associated with persons, detrimental to their moral behavior. Their parents cannot take care of their children or mistreat them.

Children suffering under any of these conditions are considered abandoned and placed under a special court *(Juizado de Menores)* equal to juvenile courts.

Another group of troubled children is made up of delinquents. An infant or juvenile delinquent is any person below 18 years who behaves as a criminal, that is, commits a crime or minor offenses *(contravencoes)*.

The Brazilian system includes a peculiar trait. Although the Brazilian constitution, as elsewhere, draws clear lines between the legislature, the Judiciary and the Executive, juvenile judges are allowed enough authority to act in the problem of troubled children on a preventive basis. Such authority is not wide enough to allow them to work on the deep causes of abandonment and delinquency, most of all on its social and economic aspects. However, a juvenile judge, in his administrative area, can, and usually does, interfere in regulating public entertainment and juvenile behavior by issuing written orders *erga omnes* covering all people below 18 years.

---

3. José Candido de Albuquerque Melo Matos—*Rules for protecting and helping abandoned and delinquent children,* 1923.

Thus, for instance, the law forbids people below 14 to frequent night shows after 8 P.M. The judge can extend this prohibition to people below 18 if he is persuaded that in his city such is the most adequate procedure for the protection of young people. Federal law prescribes an action; but the judge enacts it according to his best knowledge. Both measures, however, apply to everybody and create obligations.

A new law is now under scrutiny by the National Congress. It was specially written and approved by the National Associaion of Juvenile Judges. Following the recent Belgian and Portuguese models, it dismissed the labels applied to juveniles such as "abandoned" and "delinquent" or "law breakers." A general term, "irregular condition," will be applied to all youth below 18 who:

- suffer from material deprivation through their parents or tutors' deliberate intervention or omission;
- are victimized by any kind of ill treatment carried against them by parents or tutors;
- are under moral risk by frequenting disreputable places;
- are not able to be represented before courts;
- are singled out as deviants through maladjustment to family or community;
- have been arrested as law breakers *(infratores)*.

As to the treatment of the "irregular conditions," judges can, according to the prospective code, apply measures to eliminate the problem by placing the juvenile in his own or a substitute family or placing him in a specialized establishment. The placement in a substitute family is done through the so-called guardianships *(guardas)*, which may be definite or temporary, by adoption and by adopted legitimacy.

Internment is resorted to only when it is not possible to place the child in a home. This measure has a transitional character, since the courts continue to try to place him in a family.

9

Once the child is considered in an "irregular condition" every measure depends on a judicial decision which might place him under the control of the Public Counsel, after examination and approval from experts, mostly social workers.

The law breakers, either criminals or minor offenders, are brought to the juvenile courts. They are divided into two groups: below 14 and between 14 and 18 years. The first are not submitted to legal procedures, and a decision is immediately reached upon the police investigation.

Those between 14 and 18 are brought to judgement and have to pass through measures of reeducational treatment according to the following rules. If they are not considered dangeous, the judge can return them to their tutors' custody, or have them interned in an educational establishment for any length of time. If they are considered dangerous, the judge can send them to an appropriate esablishment until they are no more considered a social risk.

The criteria for determining whether or not he may represent a danger, is reached through the examination of motives and circumstances related to the youth's deviant behavior as well as the offender's general attitude according to an evaluation made by an interdisciplinary team.

In Brazilian law, an article of utmost importance commands that once a person has reached the age of 21 years, and he is still considered dangerous, the juvenile judge must deliver him to the criminal judge to be interned in a penitentiary. The latter will determine if he should be placed apart from adult criminals in the hope that he might be returned to a social life. Thus, the offender is viewed as a sick person and since he is not sentenced, can return to community life after being considered in a state of good recovery. During the internment, every effort will be made to bring about his social reintegration.

Probation was incorporated into the juvenile code in 1927 and was applied to all juveniles who were released from establishments. The new code replaces probation with "supervised release." Supervised freedom consists not only in keeping watch over the delinquent juvenile but in helping him to return to his community. This system has been already adopted by some juvenile's judges in the country. In 1971 the Juvenile Court in Rio de Janeiro, under Judge Alyrio Cavalieri, created a special Department of Supervised Release which, besides the purpose of following the juvenile law-breakers after release from penal establishments, would also supervise deviants, even though the latter had not been through legal procedures.

In 1971, its first year, 117 juveniles who had not been brought to court, passed through the Department. They were the so-called "spontaneous." Among them, 82 presented involvement with drugs. They were between 10 and 17. During their stay in the Department, important observations were compiled related to their behavior and the type of drug they had used. Of 196 youths who had used drugs, 178 had been through hard drugs (cocaine, LSD, amphetamines). However, no instance was found of a juvenile who had reached the "hard" phase, without previously having used marijuana. Although it cannot be definitely stated that marijuana will always lead to hard drugs, it was nonetheless clear to the Department officials that no one had begun to use hard drugs without previous experience with marijuana. However, no case was found of heroin addiction. In 1977 1,388 cases were registered related to keeping weapons without license (70), driving without a license (only those older than 18 can drive cars in Brazil) (42), intentional homicides (30), nonintentional homicides (traffic accidents) (9), aggression with body damages (109), unintentional body damages through traffic accidents (50), stealing (512), robbery (295), assault (10), sex crimes (67), drug addiction (125) and other less apparent. [4]

A sociological survey carried out in Rio de Janeiro tried to draw the profile of the juvenile delinquent, by relating the criminal act and social status. In crimes against property (thefts, robberies) the average age of the offenders is 16 years; their level

---

4.   Alyrio Cavalieri, *Direito do Menor,* 1978.

of education is semi-literate. They lack both education and work. They live in the city outskirts or the slums. The drug addicts are 16 to 17 years. They are in high school and usually do not work. Their area of residence is high-middle and middle class, their type of housing, the fashionable or average three-room apartments.

Although the study has covered every area of delinquency only these two types of offenses were published.[5]

In summary, the new Juvenile Code is a more flexible legal instrument which incorporates many innovations:

1. Avoidance of labeling troubled children with such terms as "abandoned" or "law breaker" and substituting the term "irregular condition."

2. Among the juveniles to be placed under the Judge's authority, are included those who do not have a definite legal status.

3. Some children whose behavior is deviant will be given the protection of the court.

4. There will be no payment of fees in Juvenile's Courts.

5. Childrens cases will be heard without publicity, except in the case of disappearace.

6. The clinical treatment of certain juveniles is placed under the authority of the courts.

7. Introduction of new techniques in troubled children's care such as supervised release, counseling and specialized treatment.

8. The court's focus will be family oriented.

9. Amendment of adoption laws in order to increase protection to juveniles in matters of inheritance.

---

5. Paulo Fernando Cavalieri, Michel Misse, et al.—*Juvenile delinquency in Guanabara: A Sociological Introduction* (Rio de Janeiro, 1973).

10. Vocational training will be required for public officials who work with troubled children.

11. Application of penalties to parents such as admonitions, fines and enforcement of interruption or withdrawal of parent authority (*pater potestas*), besides the duty to place the deviant son on treatment, under the threat of contempt of court.

12. Enforcement of the juvenile's right to religious assistance, according to his faith, in all the educational and penal institutions where he is placed.

13. Bearing in mind juveniles' interest, the tension of the prevalence rule in the juveniles' law above all others in any judicial decision.

3. THE SOCIAL ANGLE

The most difficult social problem Brazilians must solve is the fate of abandoned children. Until recently, it was erroneously taken for granted that the country's development, *per se*, would solve it.

To begin with, of the 110 million people living in Brazil, 58.3 million are below 19; they represent 53 percent of the total population.[6] The 14 million deprived children called *carentes* by FUNABEM represent 40 percent of the total population below 19. These data, however, have to be viewed with caution since they express poverty but not necessarily abandonment, still less deviance. The latter, according to recent estimates involve 2 million children. Since abandonment or deviance is only counted when children are rescued from poverty by, or come as problems, to social agencies, these estimates also cannot be taken as completely accurate.

6.   IBGE—*Brazilian Census,* 1970.

Thus, bare facts—no matter what might be said for or against recent estimates—lead to the conclusion that the problem is too big to be dealt with only by the government. This is to be stressed since in a paternalistic-minded country, everybody expects everything from the government. Thus the major agency that is responsible for abandoned children in Brazil is the National Foundation for Children's and Youth Welfare (Fundaçao Nacional do Bem Estar do Menor) better known as FUNABEM. It was established in December 1964. Its main purpose, according to its statute, is to preserve children's and family rights; to develop programs and to take initiatives aimed at integrating children and youth in the community; to supply the physical and moral defficiencies of their family environment; to stimulate adoption; to place the abandoned children in foster homes; to promote coordination of national agencies engaged in the children's welfare; and to offer technical assistance to the states, municipal and public agencies in the same field. In order to understand the importance of the last responsibility, it should be remembered that Brazil is a Federation, and FUNABEM, as a Federal agency, can only act in states when its intervention is asked for. Actually, since the states, with a few exceptions, lack resources to cope with the problem, FUNABEM cooperation is quite welcome.

FUNABEM acts through several programs. (1) Educational units are located in the State of Rio de Janeiro and Minas Gerais, where new techniques, methods, and procedures aiming at treatment of abandoned children or deviants are developed. They can house 2500 children per year. (2) Vocational training is provided by the Division of Vocational Training, Adoption Unit, and Division of Family Support. They can teach 8000 children per year. (3) A system of 237 private agencies in every state of the union are paid to train children sent by FUNABEM. They can take 8800 children. (4) A system of 21 state agencies for children's welfare administer programs, similar to those developed by FUNABEM, to overcome conditions of poverty.

14

The year capacity in treatment programs is 298,000; in the preventive programs 242,000. (5) FUNABEM cooperates with State Agencies for Children's Welfare and 2700 private agencies, to shelter 70,000 children. (6) A training program has been established at a special center in Rio, where people either from FUNABEM or the state agencies are trained and retrained for the special programs. Last year, the center trained 699 professionals. Between 1973, date of its inception, and 1977, it trained 3,074 experts and supervisors.

Data collected by FUNABEM give an idea about the expansion of its programs. In 1973, 28,000 children and youth went through the preventive programs and in 1978, 242,024. In 1973, 105,770 went through the treatment programs and in 1978, 290,000. It amounted to a total of 134,070 in 1973, as compared with 532,024 in 1978, a 297% increase in total attendance. In 1978, 2,484 children entered the FUNABEM units and 2,647 left. A total sum of US $875 were applied in agreements with private agencies which received 1,885 children in Rio. The Vocational Training Agency took care of 879 children in 1978. In the process, it trained professionals and sent them to work in industry and the armed forces. The Educational Division acted as supervisor of teaching offered by private establishments and extended vocational courses to 2293 in several occupations.

FUNABEM plans to expand all these programs in 1979 and to introduce new ones such as an evaluation unit for PLIMEC and the recruitment of volunteer help. Its aim is to mobilize 24,000 volunteers by 1981.

FUNABEM budget is around US $145,000, but the agencies' activities are hampered by inflation (42 percent in 1978). The *per capita* cost of internment in law-breaking cases, is US $125, and it keeps rising. For this reason, FUNABEM has been searching for new approaches beside the classic, individual treatment in institutions. Prevention has been its purpose, but it still remains a very complex affair involving government, community, and business. It depends on a national effort but it has elicited response only in a few areas of the country where a more balanced type of development has taken place, and where, due either to tradition or social development, there is a pattern of community solidarity and self-help.

By prevention FUNABEM means to improve the bio-social conditions of childhood. The first is to improve the mother's care and nutrition. The Foundation's preventive program (PLIMEC) is aimed at strengthening family conditions and at improving quality of life. PLIMEC presupposes a concerted action between children (or youth), family and community. Still, the agency is the chief promoter of this joint action and the main fund-raiser and leader. A system of agreements cements the relations between state, county, and the local agencies and acts as recipient of the funds from the federal government.

Within such limitations, the programs can be diversified according to the state agencies and the age group they chose, as their preferential goal. However, local coordination is assured by the program's structure to avoid duplication, and waste of resources. In São Paulo, for instance, the State Secretary of Health takes care of mothers' nutrition in the phase of pregnancy and covers the infant's needs up to 18 months. When he has reached this age the child comes under the responsibility of the State Secretary of Social Promotion and receives nourishment until he is six years old. A diet is planned that is conducive to a healthier development. Social Promotion has placed 300 posts in the poorest areas in the State of São Paulo. It is planned to have 300,000 infants covered by the program in 1979.

When he becomes six years, and enrolls in school, the child becomes a recipient of the State Secretary of Education for the lunch program which covers all state public schools. This program was created by FUNABEM but only in the state of São Paulo. However, the states of Minas Gerais, Bahia and Paraná are starting to implement it in their territories.

As can be noticed the program is centered on nutrition and relies heavily on public agencies and public funds. In the wealthier states, as those mentioned, there is a good chance that

16

community, business, and local leadership will get involved and might contribute to it. The problem remains in the under-developed areas of the country, in the outskirts of cities, in rural areas in the northeast and the Amazon valley, where levels of living are lower. However, the states and local units lack resources to cope with the problem and depend heavily on federal resources and programs.

The Federal programs have a wide scope. On the other hand, FUNABEM and FEBEMs concentrate on the abandoned children, or those who are born out of wedlock or from a common law marriage; or their parents have divorced or separated; their mothers are single, live as domestic servants or have become prostitutes (or both); they have lived with relatives or indifferent people. They are insecure; they carry worms, suffer from malnutrition, and are anemic. They do not show any interest in school work (supposing there are enough schools to receive them); their language is poor. They are frustrated, and their behavior is aggressive. They then may become deviant or start breaking the law.

This profile does not describe the exceptions: the child who lives apparently a normal middle-class family life but suddenly falls into a form of delinquency, small theft, car theft, reckless driving, or drug addiction and even traffic violations. In other words, chances are higher that an abandoned child from poor parents will become a social problem but there is no direct cause-effect relationship. Variables are too complex to isolate and all efforts to separate them and build new hypotheses, having in view a certain amount of prediction, have proved precarious and unsuccessful.

The policy of FUNABEM has been, in the case of abandoned children, to shift from institutional solutions, and the so-called "treatment," to non-institutional and preventive measures. However, the Foundation is supposed to receive in its establishments, willing or not, children sent by juvenile judges, who are not usually equipped with personnel and resources to discriminate between "hard" and "soft" cases. The result is that the agency is always receiving many children who should not be interned at all; but it also hosts youths who may later become dangerous criminals, and in fact have become.

FUNABEM has improved its facilities with general and vocational schools and staffed with a team of educators, sociologists, psychologists and psychiatrists, as well as training them to work in an interdisciplinary methodology. All this does not preclude eventual failures in diagnosis which result in evasion or misdemeanor. The press exploits these failures but so far, nobody has come up with a better system within the same budget and the same human resources.

It is well known that, paradoxically, it is difficult for a Brazilian couple to adopt children legally. However, in some Brazilian homes,—high, middle, or low class—children temporarily or permanently, "live with the family." "Adoption"—in the social sense, is widely practised, whereas legal adoption is hindered by an array of requirements.

Taking due notice of all these problems, FUNABEM started in 1977 an adoption program by opening an agency in Rio de Janeiro. The program covers children considered by the juvenile judge as abandoned; and families interested in adopting a child. From all the children sent to public nurseries by the judge, those are selected for the adoption program who, after careful observation, prove healthier. The others are returned to their original families or sent to another institution.

The candidates who wish to adopt a child have to fill the legal requirements. They must be older than 30 years, married for five years, to be at least 18 years older than the adopted, to agree to be the legal representative of the child in the case he is legally incapable or newly born.

During its short experience the agency has observed traits which usually do *not* recommend a candidate. The candidate should not be above 51 years. He should not adopt a child if there is a conflicting family situation or to overcome the loss of a child; intention to fill engagements (*cumprir promessas*) with saints and holy people—a type of religious behavior very usual in popular cults; simulated pregnancy; rejection due to non-ful-fillment of psycho-social requirements established by the program such as stable personality, normal life, etc.

Specific places have been set up to handle applications, which has opened up new possibilities to people who otherwise would not even know how to handle the legal procedures. As a public agency, FUNABEM cannot evade the strict rules set by law and the court's instructions. The gap between "social" and legal adoption is still wide, but to reverse the situation will be only possible after drastic changes in the law.

After considering each application the program's social worker proceeds to a social evaluation of the candidate; then a psychological evaluation is also made. Only after the candidate is judged mentally and socially sound is he introduced to the child. Once an agreement has been reached between the candidate, the child, and the social worker, the child is released to the candidate for a probationary period of at least 60 days. After the follow-up, the program's team sends its conclusive approval (or refusal) to the judge, asks him to release the child from the nursery, and to delegate a provisional guardianship, after which adoption is granted.

From its implementation in September 1977 to August 1978 the agency selected a total of 522 candidates, 300 of which were considered eligible (59 percent). Most of the eligible (34 percent) became interested in adoption less than a year before applying to the agency. The motives presented by the candidates ranged from incapacity to bear children (54 percent) to impossibility to have more children (21 percent), feeling of loneliness (7 percent), need to aid a child (8 percent), to attend request of only child (2 percent), not wishing to have children due to the fact of being single (2 percent). Others wanted to adopt a particular child to pay an obligation (*promessa*). Some wished to have a daughter, or a son specifically, or did not wish to have biological children. Some wanted to give legal status to a *de facto* adoption or even to have someone to leave social security benefits (4.5 percent).

Most of the eligible candidates (67 percent) come from the city's industrial middle-class area, but others are from the neighboring industrial and satellite cities (15 percent), or from other towns (24 percent). Only 7 percent are from the residential areas.

Most of the candidates, in general women, work at home (39 percent). Army personnel (5 percent), clerks (4 percent), workers (4 percent), drivers (4 percent), housekeepers (4 percent), public clerks (3.5 percent), industrialists (3 percent), and others non-specified (32 percent) make up the applicants' occupations. The great majority of married parents were in the 30 to 35 (49 percent) and 35 to 40 age brackets (40 percent) although men predominated in the first group and women in the second. Women also predominated in the age bracket below 30 and in the group between 45 and 50. Most, of course, were married (80 percent). Singles were represented by 4.5 percent, widowers by 2 percent, separated by 2 percent and common law marriage couples— a peculiar feature of Brazilian lower and lower middle class, 12.5 percent.

Most of them (46 percent) earned between three and nine minimum salaries (about US $234 and US $697 at the time).

As to the children they wanted to adopt, applicants seem to prefer male white children below one year for their first choice, then negro, then mulatto.

4. CONCLUSIONS

It is a matter of simple good sense that a national policy for children's and youth's welfare cannot be handled, to say the least, by isolated areas of the administration. Unless the whole body of government is imbued of the problem's importance and priority, efforts, no matter how well financed and far reaching, remain scattered and pointless.

In Brazil, besides FUNABEM, a vast array of agencies takes care of the troubled children's plights. Each focuses on a given aspect of the problem: health (Health Ministry and the Social Security System); nutrition (National Institute for Food and Nutrition, INAM); legal (Ministry of Justice, the State Secretaries of Justice and several agencies dealing with legal administration, legal tutors, public prosecutors, curators, etc.); education (Ministry of Education through several departments, state secretaries of education and the corresponding municipal agencies); labor (Ministry of Labor and the corresponding State Secretaries).

To these public agencies we must add the Church and a vast array of private social and educational institutions. It is apparent that national, state or local bureaucracies cannot handle the problem adequately without the help of private initiative. Within Brazil, however, the latter is only called upon by the administrators to supply funds, not as a partner in a system oriented by the same values, in the framework of a broad national policy.

In order to cope with a problem of such magnitude we need more than a coordination of separated agencies or episodic campaigns to raise funds and to attack a "social problem." All this might be helpful, but it must be tied up to structural changes such as a definite intervention in land ownership, in income distribution, in urban planning, and a policy of job creation.

Most of all, the whole program of children's and youth's welfare should turn around a national policy for family aid. Strange as it may seem, in a country where the fulcrum of society is the family, there is no agency to help or protect families in distress. Although the government has claimed to have boosted social development, it is still tacitly understood as a congeries of programs which scatter large resources in a paternalistic context. Social security programs are always aimed at individuals, and their recent shift towards computerized massification did not improve the situation.

Poverty, mostly in underdeveloped areas, either rural or urban, needs a broader attack which official agencies are unable or insufficient to promote. A lot more should be done through community leadership, at least where it has proved strong enough to carry on social development programs.

The old approach—to wait for the miracles of economic development—is both erroneous and anti-economical. To save children—from premature death, from poverty, from crime—is to build the future of the country upon its sounder source of wealth.

2

Denmark

Erik Munch-Petersen

Denmark, like other Scandinavian countries, provides a comprehensive child care system of services. The Danes have followed the road of child welfare boards rather than juvenile courts and see no need to change their direction in this regard. As the reader will see in this chapter, children's rights are not overlooked and administrative decisions are subject to appropriate appeal. While this system of juvenile justice has been criticized in some areas its advocates remain convinced that it stigmatizes less, that dangers of courtroom drama and trauma are reduced by the exercize of this reasonable informality and that its positive results have been proven by time. The term "social judge" is used, not paradoxically, but to indicate that the authority of the state does exist but that it is applied, not adversarily, but as an exercize in joint responsibility between the state and parents. Social Judge Munch-Petersen is an international authority on Child Welfare and his appraisal of the Danish system should be required reading for social workers and judges alike.

Editor

BACKGROUND

At the turn of the century Denmark like other Scandinavian countries, introduced a system of welfare committees to deal with cases of maladjusted children and young persons.

The background to this system was much the same as led other Western European and North American countries to establish juvenile courts. In those nations it was felt that the way in which children were treated in ordinary criminal courts and institutions for criminals was inhuman and inadequate. But the Scandinavian countries chose to establish the committees rather than juvenile courts. One of the reasons was probably that Scandinavia at that time introduced a rather high minimum age of criminal responsibility (15 in Denmark and Sweden, 14 in Norway) and that it was considered important to get the children out of the ordinary penal system by granting more and more responsibility to local authorities. In the light of this, it was felt natural to include laymen on a voluntary basis in the problems of rehabilitating children and young persons.

The Childrens Act of 1905 was passed, which introduced an entirely new authority, the so-called *"Protection Board."* This board was entitled to decide whether measures should be taken to intervene in the upbringing of children and, if so, what measures to take. At least one board was set up in each government area with representatives of teachers and clergymen, and in some areas doctors. In the cities the chairman of the board was a lawyer.

Originally the power of the local boards was limited because decisions for the placing of children in residential care were to be approved by a central government agency, the National Protection Board, one of the members of which had to be a judge or a former judge. Gradually the local boards were given more responsibility. According to the *Childrens Protection Act, 1922* the local boards could make decisions themselves to remove children from their homes and decide where to place them. The National Board generally only acted as an appeals board. The composition of the local boards was altered, too. Board members

24

were no longer required to have any special qualifications since the local protection board was considered a part of the local popular self-government system. But still a lawyer had to be present, when more important decisions were to be taken.

The Social Reform Act of 1933 linked the local boards more closely to the politically elected local community councils through special *child welfare committees.* The majority of the members had to be members of the community councils as well. But some members with special experience in child welfare could be added. The amendments of 1958 and 1964 to this act (The Care of Children and Young Persons Act) were founded on the same principles. The child and youth welfare committee members were still elected by the local community councils, but only the chairman of the social committee of that council was required to be a member of the child and youth welfare committee.

The main principles of The Care of Children and Young Persons Act were that all child and youth welfare was to be considered to be part of a family policy with the aim of assisting parents in the upbringing of their children. Children were to be regarded as part of their family, and the child and youth welfare committee was to cooperate with all other public agencies such as the school and health sector and the police. *The Social Assistance Act, 1974* stressed the idea even more that the family should be treated as a unity and only be assisted by one local authority. One of the consequences of this was that the special child and youth welfare committees were abolished and their powers transferred to the local *Social Welfare Committee* of the community council.

In each local government area a social welfare committee is set up under the provisions of the Local Government Act. According to these rules, the local community council will elect the committee members from among its members. In local-authority areas with a municipal corporation, to which the administration of social affairs is entrusted, matters relating to social assistance shall be handled by the corporation.

The social welfare centers set up by the county councils give the social welfare committees guidance and make experts available to the committees. The Minister of Social Affairs is the supreme administrative authority in matters of social assistance and formulates regulations as necessary in the field, assisted by the National Social Welfare Office.

The social welfare committee must grant assistance to a person according to his *need* whatever might be the cause of that need. The committee may offer single persons as well as families continuing *advice and guidance,* even on its own initiative. The purpose of such services shall be to help people overcome any immediate difficulties and, in the long run, to enable them to resolve, by their own efforts, their underlying problems. The advice and guidance may be given alone or in connection with other help or assistance.

As far as *children and young persons* are concerned the law gives the social welfare committee special responsibilities. Thus Section 32 of the Act makes it the duty of the committee to supervise the conditions under which children within its area live and to support the parents in their upbringing and care. Where a child is likely to be in need of special support the committee provides for an inquiry to be made into the conditions of the child. If necessary the committee may arrange for the child to be examined by a doctor or a psychologist, if appropriate, by referring the child to a child guidance center. The committee can give the parents special guidance and support, if the child has difficulties in relation to his daily environment, his school, or the community, or if the child is otherwise living under unsatisfactory conditions.

Where supportive measures are required *in the interests of the child* the committee may, if possible, in agreement with the child and his home, give directions or orders for the care or treatment, upbringing, education or employment of the child. The committee can appoint a personal adviser for the child or even place the child away from home. A personal adviser may be appointed where the family does not wish to receive ordinary guidance. Further, a personal adviser may be appointed for young persons over 15 years of age in connection with withdrawal of a charge or as the condition for a suspended sentence. Such measures must terminate not later than the date on which the young person attains the age of 20. Supportive measures in the case of young persons over 18 years of age, however, may be maintained or taken only if the young person consents thereto. If the parents oppose the taking of a supportive measure, as mentioned above, a decision shall be taken in a meeting of the committee; this decision may be appealed to the county appeals board.

For the *placing of children and young persons in residential care without consent* special rules are set up in Part VIII of the Social Assistance Act:

Sect. 123:(1) When absolutely essential for the welfare of the child, the local social welfare committee may, until the child attains the age of 18, without the consent of the person having the parental rights over the child resolve—
(i) to remove the child from home;
(ii) to commit the child to the psychiatric department of a hospital or to a mental hospital with the acceptance of the medical superintendent of the hospital, even though the general conditions prescribed in the legislation on hospitalisation of the mentally ill are not satisfied;
(iii) to recommit the child within two years of his being tentatively restored to his home;
(iv) to refuse restoration or place the child elsewhere, notwithstanding the fact that the initial care was established with the consent of the person having the parental rights over the child.

(2) When the young person attains the age of 18, supportive measures under section (1) may be maintained only if the young person consents thereto. Supportive measures shall however terminate not later than the date on which the young person attains the age of 20.

The Act does not specify what is meant by cases in which it must be considered "absolutely essential for the welfare of the child'' to remove it from home or refuse restoration. Some guidance is found, however, in a circular No. 191 issued by the Ministry of Social Affairs on October 9, 1975. In section 39 examples of such cases are mentioned, which were explicitly referred to in section 28 of the Care of Children and Young Persons Act of 1964: One describes cases where the child or the young person has shown considerable difficulties in adjusting to his daily surroundings, the school or society as a whole, and the parents are held to be unable to cope with the education. Another example provides cases where the child or the young person lives under such conditions that the psychic or physical health or development is or might be seriously damaged. Finally, examples are given of cases where the parents do not see to it that the child or the young person is given necessary special care or other necessary treatment of psychic or physical sufferings.

Section 7 of another circular (No. 184) of October 1, 1975 states that individual acts or omissions will generally not be sufficient cause for intervention, but a series of acts or omissions must have shown that serious problems for the child or the young person makes intervention absolutely essential. But of course a single event might be serious enough to justify intervention.

Section 124 of the Social Assistance Act stipulates that if a child has been placed away from home without the intervention of the local social welfare committee, the committee may refuse to allow him to be returned to his home if this would be contrary to the interests of the child. Also, a child may be returned to his home, after two years stay with a private family, only with the permission of the committee.

If it is decided to remove a child from his home or commit the child to a mental hospital, or if return of a child to his home is being considered, the local judge of the lower court and a psycho-educational adviser appointed by the county council must be consulted. The judge shall guide the committee as to the interpretation and application of the law and as to the evaluation of the available faces. He shall preside over the discussions and see that the necessary inquiries have been made.

The person having the parental rights over the child, the guardian, and the child or young person himself have the opportunity to make a statement to the local social welfare committee before a decision is made. They may enlist the assistance of a third party, who may appear before the committee.

If it is necessary to make a prompt decision, the chairman of the local social welfare committee is entitled to make a provisional order, but as soon as possible this order shall be brought before the committee for decision.

PROCEDURE IN CRIMINAL CASES.

As mentioned above, the minimum age of criminal responsibility in Denmark is 15 years. This means that the only competent authority to take action, if a person under 15 commits an act which would be criminal if committed by a person over 15, will be the local social welfare committee. However, the police will often become involved in such a case during the investigation of a case. The police officer may in such a case ask a representative of the social welfare committee to be present at the questioning of the child, but later the case will be transferred to the committee.

For young persons between age 15 and 18 the public prosecutor may withdraw the charge on condition that the young person is taken care of by the local social welfare committee and follows the instructions, given him by the committee. Special conditions may be added, such as placement in a welfare institution, and generally a probation period will be fixed.

In the great majority of cases, charges against persons under 18 years are withdrawn. Before the prosecutor makes his decision, the local social welfare committee will be consulted. A charge may only be withdrawn, if there is a full confession supported by the evidence of the case. The conditions for the withdrawal of the charge should be approved by the court.

CONTROL OF "LAYMEN."

In international circles, the question has often been put how

Denmark could leave important decisions, such as the placement of children in residential care without consent, to "laymen" without "judicial control."

It must be considered, however, that a fair amount of control is built into the system. For one thing, before the local Social Welfare Committee can take any decision without consent on removing a child from his home the most competent local juridical authority, the local judge of the lower court (always a lawyer), must be present and preside over the discussings and advise the committee. A specialist on child psychology is present too to give advice to the committee. For another, the National Social Appeals Board can be asked to hear all appeals against decisions taken by the local Social Welfare Committees and affirmed by the County Appeals Boards, or *direct* appeal can be made to the National Social Appeals Board. This Board consists of two lawyers (social judges) and two laymen, appointed by representative organizations. The lawyers are changed regularly, and the laymen will vary from division meeting to division meeting. Generally, a physician will be present at all meetings to advise the meeting, but without being entitled to vote.

It was felt, however, that the responsibility of making decisions without consent was so great that it was necessary to leave such decisions to a special division of the board (which also handles all other kinds of social cases to stress that child and youth welfare measures are only one part of the total social welfare system). It is therefore stated in the standing order of the board, that the two social judges should be the same in all cases, and in practice the first two judges were the former president of the National Board of Child and Youth Welfare and his deputy. The laymen, too, should have special experience in the child and youth welfare field. It is laid down, too, in the standing orders, that a specialist in child psychiatry or in psychology shall always be present at the meeting of this division and (without a formal vote) advise the members of the division.

If it is felt desirable to hear the parents or the young people, they will be asked to appear at the meeting of the board, and a request from the parents or the young persons to express their views on the case directly to the board members will always be accepted. They are allowed to appear with anybody to assist them, but at present, there are no provisions to pay for legal aid.

Sometimes when the board thinks that a case is not sufficiently investigated, the board may send its special inspector to investigate the case at the spot.

Finally, the special division of the National Social Appeals Board still has special powers. Thus if the local social welfare committee does not carry out the necessary inquiries or fails to take supportive measures, as required, the county appeal board or the national social appeals board may make a resolution in the matter and order the committee to carry out the resolution. This means, that the social appeals board (and in urgent cases the social judge of the child welfare division) may make decisions to remove a child from his home or refuse restoration, when such a decision is considered absolutely essential for the welfare of the child.

For many years it was considered quite natural in Denmark that the decisions taken by the local protection boards or child welfare committees and affirmed by the administrative National Appeals Board were final. No appeal could be made to the ordinary courts. In 1953, however, an amendment was made to the Danish constitution which stated, that apart from the area of criminal procedure, any administrative decision on deprivation of liberty might be tried by the ordinary courts or other judiciary. As decisions on removals of children from their homes without consent and refusals of restoration at that stage were considered to be deprivation of liberty, an act was passed in 1954 introducing the possibility to appeal the decisions of the National Appeals Board to the ordinary local lower court. However, this caused some difficulties because, in most of these cases the same judge had already acted as judicial adviser to the child welfare committee, before it made its decision. Consequently the whole problem was considered by a government committee. This committee discussed, too, whether child welfare provisions without consent could in fact be considered to be deprivation of liberty, as the child under parental authority had no liberty to decide where it wanted to be, and the deprivation could only consist of a decision, regulating the parents right to decide where the child should be or the child's right to be brought up with his parents. These—rather academic—problems were not solved, but it was held that such serious intervention in family life was important enough for it to be treated as if it were deprivation of liberty with the consequence that there should be a possibility to have the administrative decisions tried by the ordinary courts.

The amendments of 1958 of the Social Reform Act therefore stated that the decisions without consent of the National Appeals Board could be appealed directly to the high courts of justice, of which there are two in Denmark. While the high court generally in civil cases works in divisions, consisting of three lawyers, these cases were considered so special that it was found advisable to assign a specialist in child welfare and a specialist in child psychiatry or in psychology.

The high court acts as a *civil* court, and the purpose of the oral proceedings is to decide whether the provisions for action without consent, laid down in the Social Assistance Act, are applicable or not. The court is not only working as a court of cassation but is entitled to try the whole case. In principle, the court must accept or reject the decision, taken by the welfare committee and affirmed by the National Board. In practice, however, the high court (like the National Appeals Board) often assumes a mediating function and in several cases tries to make the parents accept the recommendations of the welfare agencies, if the court finds these measures necessary.

The court may decide that the case shall be heard in camera, and in all cases no mention of the name, occupation, or address of the persons involved may be made in any public report of the court proceedings or of the judgment.

The parents are given free legal aid, and in special cases, where the interests of the child and the interests of the parent might differ, a special lawyer is appointed to look after the interests of the child.

The decision of the High Court is final, but in exceptional cases the Minister of Justice may permit an appeal to the Supreme Court.

The Social Assistance Act, 1974, in principle preserved this appeal system. The only change was that instead of the decisions of the former National Board of Child and Youth Welfare it will now be the decisions taken by the special division of the National Social Appeals Board which may be appealed directly to the High Courts.

PERSONAL EVALUATION

It is generally considered an advantage of the Danish system that all activities are concentrated in one authority: the local social welfare committee, whose chairman may act immediately in urgent cases. It is assumed that the committee—through its field workers and in cooperation with all other authorities in the local community—has an intimate knowledge of the living conditions of the children and their parents in the area and will know who are in need of special support. This should make it easier to detect when the welfare of a child is endangered so that assistance to the family can be offered. It should make it possible too to find the—very few—cases where intervention is felt necessary even if the parents do not agree.

It is considered an advantage too that people who fail to bring up their children in a proper way, are appraised by their peers in the local community acting under political responsibility. The system may, however, involve the risk that, for political reasons, a committee desists from taking an unpopular decision even when it ought to have been taken in the interests of a child.

In recent years it was argued that the whole idea of the welfare committee assisting families with an offer to help them solve their problems in bringing up their children might be compromised. That is, the same authority at a certain stage has the power to intervene in family life and even decide to take away the children from their home disregarding the protest of the parents (and the children).

The welfare workers working with the families on behalf of the committee, and making a great effort to gain the confidence of the family members, might feel frustrated too when at a certain stage (according to provisions laid down in the law) they are obliged to tell the committee that the welfare of a child is endangered if action without consent is not taken.

Some people therefore suggest that the power to make decisions without consent should be left to special boards, probably set up on the county level. At present, such suggestions have not found much support. The main obstacle to such a system is possibly that somebody must be bound to bring such a case before the special board, and having the welfare of the child in mind it would be impossible to exempt the field workers of the welfare committee and the committee members themselves from the duty to pass on their knowledge of the families to such a board. The families, therefore, might easily consider the welfare committee and its staff as police spies, and the image of the welfare authorities would remain threatened.

*　*　*

It is considered an advantage of the Danish system that children and young people are generally exempted from the jurisdiction of penal law. In practice there will very seldom be any question of establishment of guilt, and the problem whether the special conditions laid down in the law for action without consent are fulfilled is controlled rather effectively by lawyers, before the committee takes its decision, and during the appeal procedure as well.

It must be admitted, however, that the Danish system historically was built up as a system to protect *the parents* against intervention in family life on the part of the public authorities. Only the parents are asked to be present at the committee meeting and

34

to give their comments before the committee makes its decision. And only the parents are entitled to appeal to the National Social Appeals Board and later to the high courts.

It is laid down, however, in the Social Assistance Act that the child or young person shall be given the opportunity to make a statement to the local social welfare committee before a decision is made. In practice very small children are excluded, and even older children and young persons will seldom appear before the committee itself. They give their statement to a member of the staff before the committee meeting. There is a growing tendency, however, to have young people appear before the committee itself.

It is sometimes felt that more attention should be paid to the interests of the child and young person himself, and there is a growing tendency to doing so.

It is desirable that not only the parents but the children themselves feel that the local social welfare committees are there to protect their interests as well. In recent years, as a result, children and young persons approach the welfare committees themselves for assistance when they feel that their home conditions are unsatisfactory.

As mentioned above, the National Social Appeals Board still has the power to order the local social welfare committee to take supportive measures on behalf of a child or young person, if the National Board finds it necessary in the interests of the child and the local committee does not take the necessary action. Such cases are generally started by the public or by relatives, but in recent years the National Board also has received applications from young persons who in vain had tried to make the welfare committee take action on their behalf.

My personal impression is that public opinion is so critical of the work of the social welfare committees that they are very reluctant to take decisions without the parents' consent—in some cases even too reluctant when the interests of the child are to be considered.

3

Egypt

Saied Ewies

Under the Chairmanship of Professor Ahmad Khalifa the National Center of Social and Criminological Research in Cairo has earned an international reputation in all aspects of crime prevention and treatment of offenders. It was deemed highly important that "Justice and Troubled Children Around the World" should include a chapter from Egypt. Professor Ewies, Counsellor and member of the Center's faculty, has provided the following contribution, which he has entitled "Troubled Children in Egypt." It brings to the reader the perspective of ancient Egyptian history and culture. In it Professor Ewies contemplates the value of linking the urgent needs in a modern changing society with the basic tenets of traditional society. The writer points out that the rights of children, with which we are so pre-occupied today, formed the basis of discussion along the shores of the Nile as far back in history as 64 A.D. Modern juvenile justice in Egypt coincides with its appearance in other parts of the world. A chronology of Egypt's action in this area is included.

Editor

The Egyptian slogan that says that "Childhood is the maker of the future and hence the working generations are bound to ensure for it all the requirements to bear the responsibilities of successful leaderhip in the future" expresses a conviction deep in the hearts of contemporary Egyptians, handed down to them over thousands of years and originating in ancient Egyptian society.

This heritage has accommodated the teachings of Aton, some 3500 years ago, of which the main canticle says:

> you, the creator of the germ in
> >   the woman,
> who pitchforks posterity from
> >   a seed,
> letting the babe living in its
> >   mother's abdomen,
> calming it down so as not to
> >   weep,
> suckling it even in the womb,
> you who give the breath to keep life
> >   for every one you create,
> when it comes out of the
> >   womb on its delivery,
> you who open its mouth absolutely,
> and grant it the requisites of
> >   life.[1]

This heritage has been preserved since the early years of the 18th Dynasty (circa 1570 B.C.), representing the most important document handed over from the ancient world about the mettle of the Egyptian man and his progress from the moral point of view. This great and noble Egyptian believed in the concept of doomsday. It was his opinion that the soul of the deceased, before reaching the Paradise of Osiris, would go along an arduous road fraught with perils. The arrival of the soul at the "kingdom" of Osiris did not mean the end of this stage, since the soul had to pass through a very difficult test before Osiris, the God of the other world, prior to association with the other fortunates who had preceded it to paradise. The deceased had to stand trial before the court of justice in the other life to account for his deeds on earth.

On arrival at the "Hall of Truth," the soul directing its sight towards the God, should say:

Peace be upon you, the great Lord, the God of Truth, I have come to you, Lord, and was sent here to behold your Beauty—I know your name, and the names of the 42 Gods who are with you in the Hall of Truth, who thrive on the sinners by sapping their blood. On this day morals are tested before Osiris.

The soul of the deceased then enumerates the sins which he has not committed, which are numerous, implicating the people with whom the deceased has lived before his death, their various ranks and standings, and their various ages and kinds. He did not commit any vicious deed and did not inform against a servant to his masters, and he had not been the cause for the weeping of any man etc. *"And I did not usurp any milk from the mouth of a child."*[2]

I

For thousands of years, since time immemorial, the ancient Egyptian heritage has conserved a constitution which was concerned with the child's protection and on the nonusurption of its rights. This heritage also initiated concern over the child's upbringing by adequate educational methods which comply with its age, aimed at sowing the seeds of good character and wisdom. If the father wished to assuage the rigours of his advice to his son, for instance, he would play upon the word "hear" saying to him that the son who politely hears the words of those who are older than him would one day become a judge who would hear cases:

> Listening is beneficial for the
> > sons who hears,
> If hearing entered into the (ear) of
> > hearers,
> The hearer would become a
> > listening person,
> Hearing is good, the saying is
> > good, but . . .
> The hearer has a merit for
> > listening is beneficial
> > for the hearer,
> And hearing is superior to all
> > other things.[3]

The humane Egyptian cultural heritage has preserved concepts dealing with children's rights dating from the time when St. Mark propagated Christianity in Alexandria and ordained Enianos of Egypt as Archbishop in 64 A.D. The verses of the Bible glitter with these concepts and rights, beaming their light into the hearts of the Egyptian Christians until this day. Such concepts, to give some examples, have asserted that parents have to accept their children from the Lord. They have to love their children and should bring them to Jesus Christ. Parents have to train their children to follow God's teachings, make known to them God's judgments and His marvelous deeds, and order them to obey the Lord. And the parents have to bless their children, be kind to them, strive for their salvation, and support, admonish and bring them up.[4]

When the Arab army under Amr Ibn-al 'As had invaded the territory of Egypt, the climate of the Egyptian cultural society was influenced by the teachings of Islam. The Egyptian cultural heritage preserved the rulings of these teachings in connection with children's rights. These are found in the verses of the holy Koran and in the prophet's sayings and traditions.

The Prophet's sayings and traditions asserted parents' rights to their children's love and gratitude and the father's duty to develop these values in his son. The Prophet's sayings have also asserted equity among children in whatever the parents contribute to them. These sayings have further emphasized the rights of children to be trained from birth to six years. On reaching nine years each child should sleep separately. At 13 years to be beaten if he neglects any form of prayers. The Prophet's sayings have further asserted that it is the father's duty to bring up his child and to give him a decent name. The father is advised to be kind to his child and to spare no effort on his behalf.

The Moslem legislators have laid down rules governing the life of children, giving priority to their interest, rating care for children as equal to the striving in the God's cause. In the context of child care, the Moslem legislators have restored the child's right to acquire the nationality of its father to preserve its blood, and has asserted its right to custody, welfare, education, their souls, and their wealth and support for children from birth.[5]

II

Above, I have outlined what should be done for the Egyptian child concerning his upbringing by adequate educational methods which are appropriate to its age, but what should be done in theory is usually different from what is actually done. Owing to certain socio-cultural as well as economic and political factors, Egyptian society is not able to ensure for the Egyptian child at present all the requirments to bear the responsibilities of successful leadership in the future.

Egypt at the present time has about 16 million children under 15, out of a population of about 40 million. Infant and child mortality rates are extremely high. In 1972 there were 116.3 deaths per thousand births. The main causes of infant and child mortality are diseases of the digestive system (gastro-enteritis and other diarrhoeal diseases), and parasitic disease. In the 0–6 age groups, diarrhoeal diseases account for 46 percent of mortality cases. Infectious and parasitic diseases cause 29 percent of infant and 42 percent of preschool-aged children's deaths.[6]

In spite of the fact that the general educational policy has advanced remarkably towards the realization of its fundamental objectives, we find in the 15 years ending in June 1973, however, that the ratio of children enrolled in the primary stage to total compulsory school age population (6–12 years) reached about 70 percent only, of which approximately 60 percent were males and 40 percent females. That is, millions of children of this age-group did not find a place in a school.

The number of male children below 15 in the labor force is 12 percent of the total population in this group. The ratio of children in the labor force is four times more in the rural areas than it is in the urban area, mainly because most agricultural work requires child labor.[7]

Investigators of children's needs in Egypt have made the following conclusions. Rural children are more in need of help concerning not only their health, educational, and recreational problems, but they also need facilities for the development of their personalities. It is high time that the focus of attention be shifted to these children who consititute the majority of the child population in the country. Girls, generally speaking, are much less privileged than boys in many respects. Starting from the premises that Egyptian women constitute half the society, and that developing countries like Egypt need all their human resources to assist in development, more attention should be directed to girls' education by building more schools for girls in all districts, for all stages of education. The all-important role of mothers in the healthy growth of children, both physically and mentally, calls for concentrated efforts in order to arouse the social awareness of mothers and instruct them in correct child care and so-cialization. This is a priority to which all mass media and social agencies (Particularly rural clinic and social welfare units) should be geared. The large size of families—especially in rural areas—has proved to be a great hindrance in attending to children's needs and problems. Therefore, all efforts in connection with family planning and birth control must be considered as efforts to meet children's needs and should be given priority over many other plans and programs. The problem of drop-outs (whether these are children who never went to school or children who went to school but left before graduating) deserves special attention. Diagnosis of the problem as well as the introduction of educa-tional guidance and counselling services should be one of the pri-orities in an attempt to meet children's needs and problems. It has been proved that many children suffer from nutritional defi-ciencies. It goes without saying that health and nutritional prob-lems should be given appropriate consideration. Sex problems are either put aside or ignored. It is high time that they were re-solved by means of planned and well-organized programs.[8]

The facts show an alarming decline in services for Egyptian children of today. This could bring about many deficient fami-lies and broken homes, which may produce troubled children, the majority of whom may be juvenile delinquents.

Thus, in one of the studies supervised it was found that, of the juveniles charged with vagrancy in its numerous forms, 3176 (that is 79.9 percent of the total number) had no place to go except city streets and alleys; that is, they did not live in the shelter of a fam-ily. It was also found that 547 of the families in Cairo were un-able to carry out the process of the socialization of their sons and daughters, and brought charges of "beyond control" against them. That is, the number of juveniles who did not enjoy family life, our sound family life, reached 3723, out of the total of 4527 juveniles. Therefore, more than four juveniles per thousand of this age group in Cairo live without a family or in a deficient family.

It must be added that about 82.4 percent of the "beyond control" juveniles had had no previous convictions of vagrancy. This conclusion led us to question the truth of the changes their relatives brought against them. Were these juveniles actually guilty of bad conduct, as stated in the law? We are inclined to answer this question in the negative, until scientific study in the field proves the contrary. Our experience compels us to this answer, because we know that those responsible for these juveniles have proved to be unfit to play the role of good, decent parents. A case of "beyond control" may be brought against a child, for example, for the purpose of the revenge of a father on a divorced wife, or on the marriage of the juvenile's mother, as his only guardian, to another person, or because of inadequate economic conditions faced by the family.

These agencies can resort to a number of measures to correct juvenile delinquents. Thus, if the juvenile court finds a juvenile guilty, the judge may place the juvenile under probation, sending the juvenile to an educational institution, or have the juvenile treated in a psychological clinic.

Underlying the application of these measures is the belief that delinquent juveniles are a category of people who do not differ from other people who violate other laws of behavior. In other words, it is believed that these juveniles do not constitute a unique group, and that they are, before anything else, human beings who have been unlucky in their adjustment to the social circumstances which they face, and have therefore violated the penal code. It is believed that our view of law violators, including juvenile delinquents, must be brightened with the hope of their reformation and return to society. Such a view adopts a reformatory—not a punitive—treatment of these individuals.

Reformatory work in the field of juvenile delinquency is many-sided, as it is in the case of crime prevention. The most important aspects include police work, court action, the probation system, work in reformatory institutions, work in special institutions (for the feeble-minded and the like), work in psychological clinics, and the application of the after-care system.

The number of juvenile reformatories in Egypt has at present reached 26. Those institutions for juvenile delinquents who are mentally retarded have reached eight. The number of probation offices has now reached eleven.[10]

The following dates indicate when institutions and methods for dealing with juvenile delinquency were established.

The first modern juvenile legislation in Egyptian society.	1882
The first juvenile court.	1905
The first juvenile reformatory.	1907
The first psychological clinic.	1934
The first application of probation system	1940
The first observation institution.	1945
The first application of the after-care system.	1949
The first application of foster families	1957
The first juvenile police office.	1957
The first institution for juvenile delinquents who are mentally retarded.	1958

It should be noted, however, that in spite of the existence of measures which seek to prevent juvenile delinquency and those which seek to correct juvenile delinquents in Egypt today, the number of delinquents is on the increase. It has more than doubled between 1973 to 1977. In 1973, those juveniles accused of different crimes numbered 12,276. They were accused of committing 14,966 crimes, the majority of which were misdemeanors (75.8 percent) and the remainder were vagrant acts. In 1977 however, those juveniles accused of different crimes number 25,649. They were accused of committing 25,448 crimes, the majority of which were misdemeanors (89.7 percent) and the remainder were acts of vagrancy.[12]

III

To conclude, we may say that the real challenge which confronts Egyptian society in dealing with its problems—whether they are concerned with children, in general, and troubled children, in particular, or with other problems—is the difference between what is positive and sound in its cultural heritage, in theory, and what is negative and deficient in practice. It is a duality that should be objectively understood while tackling each of these problems.

Government planners do now appear to be seriously envisaging means of reversing the alarming decline in the past years of services for children. The 1978–1982 National Plan aims to allocate 4 percent of the total budget for health services—24.5 million ($62 million) in 1978 increasing to 29 million ($74 million) by 1982. The aim is to reduce child mortality by ensuring that the existing medical centers of health services and social-health units are adequately staffed and utilized to the full and to increase their number.

In education the goal of the Five-Year-Plan is to reach a 95 percent level of primary school enrolment by 1980 and to establish the minimum compulsory chool age to 15. A budget of 50.1 million $127 million) has been allocated to education in 1978 and will be raised progressivley to 73 million ($182 million) by 1982.

For these ambitious plans to bear fruit, however, there will have to be a dramatic improvement in the economic situation of the mass of the Egyptian People.[13]

REFERENCES

1. James Henry Breasted, *Dawn of Conscience,* translated by Selim Hassan (Cairo: Misr Bookshop, 1956), pp. 303–304.

2. Saied Ewies, *Immortality in Egyptian Cultural Heritage* (Cairo: Dar El Maaref Bookshop), 1966, pp. 71–73.

3. John Wilson, *Egyptian Civilization,* translated by Ahmed Fakhry (Cairo: Enahda Bookshop, 1955) p. 253.

4. Archbishop Eissozoros, *The Invaluable Pearl in the History of the Church,* 3rd ed. (Ein Shams, 1923), pp. 61–62.

5. Mohamed Salem Madkour, Research paper on child requirements in the U.A.R., unpublished study.

6. Irene Beason, "The Price of Poverty," *People* vol. 5, no. 4 (1978).

7. General Agency for Public Mobilization and Statistics, *Population and Development* (Cairo, 1973), pp. 180–181, 206.

8. National Center for Social and Criminological Research, and Unicef, *Assessment of Children's Needs in Egypt, A National Survey* (Cairo, 1974), pp. 188–189.

9. Saied Ewies, *The Broken Home and its Relation to juvenile Delinquency,* Proceedings of the lst Conference on Combating Crime of the United Arab Republic, January 2–5, 1961, (Cairo, 1961), p. 167.

10. Ministry of Social Affairs, *Social Statistics* (Cairo, 1974), pp. 122, 260, 262.

11. The National Center for Social and Criminological Research, *A Study on Juvenile Delinquency in The United Arab Republic* (Cairo, 1965).

12. Ministry of Interior, *Public Security Annual Reports* (Cairo, 1973), pp. 173–175 and (1977), pp. 178–181.

13. *The Price of Poverty.*

4

India

Akka Kulkarni

This chapter is not only a profile of juvenile justice in law and in action in Bombay but it is a sketch of the practices in the whole field of child welfare throughout India. It is written by a woman who presided over children's courts for many years and her comments are readily seen to be the outcome of great exposure to the problems of families in both rural and urban areas. However, this chapter is more than an account of social and juridical justice being administered. It is the sensitive story of a dedicated and sensitive woman at work in a vast country filled with cultural diversity, social distinctions and economic frustration. It is a hopeful statement about India and its intent to enrich the quality of life of children and young people.

Editor

THE CHILD IN TROUBLE IN INDIA

What do we mean by a child in trouble? Do we mean a child who has transgressed the laws of the land, or do we mean a child who has gone beyond the norms acceptable in his social circle, or society in general? Or do we mean a child who is physically, mentally, or emotionally handicapped? Or do we include all these among troubled children? In India, out of about 370 districts in the whole country, there are children's acts in about 197 of them. This shows eloquently the state of affairs as far as juvenile justice is concerned. Child legislation is mainly based on the English Children Acts, although it has been ammended when this was required. The children's acts are state laws. There is, for example, a Union Children's Act of 1960 in force in Delhi, and in Union Territories. Most of the acts that are in force cater for the destitute, uncontrollable, and other young offenders or delinquents. Some provide for child welfare boards which consider non-delinquent cases, and courts which consider young offenders and delinquents. Only the Bombay Children's Act deals with a fourth category, of victimized children. This includes victims of adult offences; cruelty, exploitation for begging, for immoral purposes, for rape, kidnapping, assault, prostitution, among others. According to the Bombay Children's Act a child is always dealt with by the juvenile court even if it is a case of murder and an adult by the adult court notwithstanding any other laws that may be in force. If an adult and a child are accused of committing a crime together, their cases may be separated, but they would be tried in the adult court. In other states the juvenile court will try the adult accused with the juvenile.

In some states the juvenile court consists of a bench of honorary magistrates. In others these courts have a full-time magistrate. He may be a judicial magistrate from the adult court, who sits separately on one or two days in a week to deal with juvenile cases, with or without so-called, honorary colleagues, some of whom are usually women.

In some states the juvenile court is regarded as a social institution. In other states the juvenile court is regarded as a criminal court. In any case the juvenile court is considered the most minor and unimportant Court in the judiciary system.

The treatment of children ranges from granting them understanding, compassion, sympathy, and the most scrupulous justice. The children are provided a variety of treatment to suit their individual needs. Or, the treatment may consider dealing with the child just like an adult and considering only the legal side. The causative factors and the emotional maladjustments among other considerations are disregarded. As for the places where there are no children's acts, the situation can be disastrous and horrendous.

There are only about 80 juvenile courts in India. The number of institutions both official and voluntary is also very small. In places where there is no children's act and the Reformatory Act of 1878 is still in force, there are only reformatories. In addition, many juvenile courts may have probation officers, who carry out all the necessary investigations and also supervise and make school contacts; they also have child guidance clinics with psychiatrists, psychologists, and psychiatric social workers at their disposal. There also are numerous voluntary and semivoluntary organizations that provide preventive and constructive work, and who are only too ready to cooperate with the court. However, in other states, the child may have no one to help him in any way at all. From all this, we may realize some of the difficulties involved in planning and providing social welfare services in the country. Fortunately most of the states and the central government have become more alert to it. As a result, efforts are being made to provide for the educational and social welfare, as well as public health, including family planning, prenatal and post natal treatment, medical care, and preventive medicine.

* * *

Before pointing out what is necessary to be done, to deal with juvenile delinquents, it may be useful to review the most possible and probable causes of children landing in trouble. The causes are the changing social system, changing morals and values, environmental changes, changes in systems of education, population explosion, imitation of manners and customs of other countries, and lack of civic and political knowledge.

THE CHANGING SOCIAL SYSTEM

The joint family system which was a great bulwark against deviation, has truly broken down in India, although, no doubt, it exists in remote rural areas. The reason for this breakdown is mainly economic. The joint family system could exist as long as India was an agricultural country only. Even then, the laws of inheritance which allow all sons to inherit the property of the parent equally, and even the daughters to inherit half of the sons' inheritance, leads to denigration of property and this makes it impossible to live on the land. This, in turn, leads to migration to cities, where industrialization is increasing. The men might seek and get some employment, but to get accommodation is the most difficult of tasks. This, in turn, leads to illegal occupation of land by squatters, where sanitation, water, and even the basic amenities of human life are lacking. Theft and destruction are rampant, due to a basic lack of understanding of civic responsibility and common sense. This in turn leads to dirt, disease and waste. But, the hospitals in India, particularly in the cities, needed to deal with this are insufficient. Overcrowding persists, and the medical staff is overworked and poorly paid; so the standard of treatment suffers.

The institution of the family has been affected by the Monogamy Act. When the Monogamy Act was put into effect, divorce was made legal, although lower classes always have had customary divorce and separation and have allowed remarriage among Hindus from time immemorial. But now the higher classes can also get divorced, and recently the divorce law has been amended to make divorce a little easier. Divorce raises the question of who will look after the children after a marriage has been dissolved.

MORALS AND VALUES

The preceeding paragraph leads us into the changing concept of morals and ethical values. Economic necessity has caused middle and higher class women to go to work. As a result, there is no parent to look after the children. As a consequence of this, the children do not get the proper amount of attention and loving care that they need, and they often seek to occupy themselves by indulging in dangerous or improper friendships, an unsuitable environment; an emphasis on sexual adventure is apparent nowadays, even among school children. There is a lack of proper inhibition, an easy contempt of virture, loyalty, and a derision of anything that seems to be old fashioned. In addition, even when the parents are at home, they are both tired and may become quarrelsome or nagging. The atmosphere at home becomes vitiated. The children lose respect for their parents, and stop believing in them. They seek the recognition of gangs of their own peer group which leads to organized crime or delinquency.

Although there is a law against taking a dowry, habit and custom are so difficult to change. As a result, a husband often is bought for the bride; that is what it really amounts to. The overall result is that if a man has a number of daughters, it may be difficult for him to get them all married. So some girls remain unmarried. Instead they are educated so that they can hold down jobs and help their parents as long as they are alive. And so, a "third sex," the spinster, is being created. Consider what the impression of that prospect must be on a girl from the time she begins to understand.

When you consider today's society, one of the things that leaps to the eye is a lack of religion and real belief in God. I do not mean ritual procedure. There is enough of that in our country, and it has become commercialized too. But where are the intrinsic values? The person who earns the most, or who is the richest, or the most powerful, is the person most respected and worshipped. There is no loyalty either in the home, in school, university, employment, or politics. This degenerates and corrupts people of all ages and at all levels of life and society.

ENVIRONMENTAL CHANGES

If the family moves to a town, it usually must settle in a shanty slum or in overcrowded rooms, usually as subtenants—legal or illegal. Primary schooling is free and secondary education is provided free as well if the earning of the parents is less than a certain sum annually. However, some families are so poor they cannot send the children to school and the way is open to get into trouble in gangs, picking pockets and robbing people. Breaking and smashing property also are violent acts and very satisfying. "Those lousy rich may have a house to live in, but they are at our mercy whenever we please" is the feeling the children get. These are of course fanned by agitators, political, or so called political, but it all boils down to the inner feeling of power, of being big, and making people cringe. The children also see their fathers strike, storm the management offices, and beat up their officers, and even commit murder. Some boast of getting away with it. Add to this the fact that even in the schools and universities the same tactics are used by teachers and professors or staff, and the students are also involved in the protest and violence.

Naturally, children are very receptive to impressions and they learn about violence at a very early age and become hardened to it.

Nowadays strikes by staff and students lead to postponed examinations, irregularities in conduction of examinations, anxiety neurosis regarding joining further courses of learning and knowledge, and fatigue. The standards or criterion of most universities have gone down. In fact some have become notorious. Copying, dishonesty, falsifications of all kinds have flourished. How does a child keep out of trouble under such circumstances?

When one realises that in this vast democracy every adult irrespective of his mental or emotional state has a vote one can visualise the tremendous potentiality for good or bad that this can be. The Indian villager or townsman is shrewd enough, and he does not lack commonsense, but violence or greed can sway him to do the opposite of what he really wants to do. A long domination by a succession of conquerors, benign or otherwise, has made this possible and thirty years of independence cannot wipe out the effects of centuries. In addition, a sense of civic responsibility is also missing, though the Indian certainly does not lack in intelligence.

Having considered these factors, we now turn to imitation of Western ideas and manners. Imitation of good things is useful, but imitation of bad or wrong things, of course, is not. For instance, drugging for kicks in the presence of European Hippies, is a nauseating sight seen in many cities now. There are brothels for girls, and for boys or young men, who cater to homosexuals. It is true that girls and young boys are brought to cities with the lure of lucrative jobs and then sold to brothels by agents. But the terrible perversions that seem to be common in the West nowadays, do not appear to be common here in the same way.

What is a child, whose father is always away, to do? Even in the villages, life has changed considerably. Decentralization of power by making the village *surpanch* the head of the village and the *zilla parishad* (local councils) responsible for most of the administration is certainly sound and good in principle. The trouble is, that sometimes the people voted into power are often the most violent, crude, and even lawless in that area, which, of course, impresses the young to become the same.

What does a child do when his parents are away from morning till night? Their children are poor in love. No servants however good or efficient, can take the place of parents; neither can any institution however superior it might be.

The causes of deviant behavior are innumerable, in fact different in the case of each child. I have merely touched on a few. The common factors in all the cases, however, are insecurity, no loving kindness, and no sense of belonging. What are the results? Briefly they may be assessed as follows. Troubled children become troubled adults, who comprise troubled countries. In a troubled country, which means most countries in the world, children become precocious, worshippers of unhealthy gods, respecting unhealthy norms, indifferent and inhumane. They have not been taught to differentiate between evil and good, between truth and falsehood, or, if they have been taught so, their parents, teachers, friends, have not set themselves as examples of the same, or have acted countrary to their own teaching, with the result that the concept of good and evil has ceased to have any meaning.

Now, looking on the other side, we must state that never has India taken such a good look at its child population. Never before has there been such an interest in children as has begun in recent years. Never such planning, or most important of all, such budgeting for preventive measures as now. For instance, rural clinics and dispensaries have been opened to provide maternity care, and homes for prenatal and postnatal help free as well as child care and nutrition centers. Schools and scholarships also have been established. The government is also taking a good look at its child labor laws, and is planning for their revision. There is no doubt that people are aware of the problem of juvenile justice and that they are struggling to solve them. This is a most hopeful state of affairs. But, just as Rome was not built in a day nor can India. It will take time, and years and years of hard genuine effort, planning and enforcing work. That day will certainly dawn, but how long it will take, one cannot say.

Love our children with true love, not sentimentality. Let us discipline ourselves, so that we can realize their true value and importance, and see that we "do not lead them into temptation," but with the grace of God "deliver them from evil, Amen."

5

Israel

David Reifen

In this chapter Dr. Reifen, former Chief Judge of the Juvenile Courts in Israel, describes the social services in his country. He sees the Juvenile Court as a therapeutic force in the community and emphasized the need for judges to be specially trained, not only in law but also in the social sciences, to deal with the judiciable problems of children and families. With Israel's decision to extend the jurisdiction of the court from 16 to 18 years and to raise the age of criminal responsibility from 9 to 12 years new areas of community responsibility have appeared. Israel has special problems and its whole social service delivery system has been created to meet these needs. The reader will be interested in the use of special youth interrogators who interview child witnesses and act as their surrogates in court thus sparing those of tender years the traumatic effect of court room proceedings and cross-examination. To get a more comprehensive picture of Israel's way of dealing with its troubled children the reader should become acquainted with Dr. Reifen's book *The Juvenile Court in a Changing Society* published by the University of Pennsylvania Press in 1972.

Editor

HISTORICAL PERSPECTIVE

Since the establishment of the State of Israel in May 1947, the population has been more than trebled by an influx of immigrants from numerous and widely differing countries. There are now approximately three and a half million inhabitants in Israel, among them 12 percent non-Jews, mostly Moslem Arabs. The major effort within the Jewish population has been concerned with the absorption of large masses of people which has been taking place for the last 30 years. Under prevailing circumstances this has entailed a heavy strain on economic as well as socio-cultural development, which enhanced difficulties in the process of integration. Suffice it is to mention that this process occurred within a small territory and within a brief period of time. Invariably, immigration to Israel has meant for many, and particularly for those who have come from Asia, North Africa, and countries of the Near and Middle East, a transplantation into competitive society, which is urbanized and industrialized on the pattern of countries in the western hemisphere. This sudden change has tended to disrupt the ordinary way of life of individuals, of families, and of whole groups. They have been thrown out of their normal rhythm and have encountered difficulties in reorienting themselves to the rhythm of the new environment.

We witness a clash of culture with all its inherent consequences. This process is expecially felt among the various oriental communities as compared to their counterpart, namely those who have immigrated from European countries.

Those who originate from the oriental countries have increased numerically to about half of the Jewish population in Israel. Thus a radical change in the distribution of the various ethnographic groups has taken place during the last 30 years. A conspicuous feature has been observed that, there were not many Jews from these Oriental countries who have had experience in manual labor. They have also had almost no training in, or knowledge of, technical matters, and a systematic process of education was largely foreign to them. In Israel all these are basic requirements, and they confer upon individuals, as well as on a particular ethnic group a specified social status. For many who have come from these countries it means that, on their part special efforts have to be made to gain such status, whereas the government is challenged with an enormous task to make appropriate provisions to reach this target.

Immigration to Israel has also meant a change from a society with strong taboos concerning social contacts and modes of behaviour to a society in which no such taboos exist. It became of decisive importance that in this situation the values of the family were immediately effected, and the changes that took place within the family unit were often most painful. Furthermore, the characteristic structure of the family of oriental Jewish communities gives the father unquestioned authority. This status becomes of particular importance in the new environment in Israel, where many of the values and customs hitherto accepted by them are looked upon from entirely different angles. Arising out of this situation, the whole family structure is subjected to strong ambivalent feelings and anxieties. For the father it means often to fail in keeping pace with the demands of the new society. In most instances he is the main provider of the family, and it was natural that he has had the main say in all family matters. Even in instances in which he was not the main breadwinner, the father was still regarded in high esteem by the mere fact of being the head of the family. Because of immigration to Israel he was unable to remain the provider of the family, because of his inability to keep pace with the requirements of a competitive society like that of Israel. In addition his lack of general knowledge in a society in which such knowledge is the most important yardstick for a recognized social status, has led to a decreasing influence. In the new environment children often know better than the father, and many depend on their children to interpret the new environment to them. These are a few examples of situation which cause fathers feelings of inadequacy, frustrations and anxiety.

Similar changes, although of a different nature can be observed in the status of mothers. Equality of sexes has become a matter of course for women in many countries of the Western world. In Israel, such status has been very pronounced for many years. For those coming from oriental countries, however, it is quite a different matter. The mere fact of going to work outside the home, of meeting men and women freely in factories, workshops, and other places of work, has enhanced the status of women and has thus brought about an enormous change in the pattern of life of many families. Some ethnographic groups of oriental origin have, soon after their arrival in Israel, prevented females of the family to accept jobs outside their own home, because of fear lest such a step might interfere with old established tradition. Others, from similar background have adopted a more liberal attitude. Circumstances have forced the former group to give up much of their resistance and to give way, reluctantly, to modes of behaviour in the new environment. Among all groups such changes have given rise to anxieties and emotional upheaval. Ambivalent feelings have ensued which have resulted in lack of security. They may suddenly become either more lenient or more strict in handling and educating their children. Their upbringing becomes confused.

The confusion is illustrated by an instance which I had to handle in the Juvenile Court in Tel-Aviv. A boy aged 12 years was tried in Court for the third time. He came usually with his mother, but I felt that the matter should be discussed with his father as well. When I asked the father how he explained the delinquent behaviour of his boy he said: "When I was still in Morocco, I knew what was right and wrong, and my family obeyed me. Here I know nothing. My wife interferes in things, which she would not have done at home, and she thinks she knows better than I do." After some further conversation between us he added: "When the police came home with the boy and asked me to certify that the boy would appear in court when summoned to do so, the policeman immediately added, 'But don't beat him because of this.' Now you see, even the police are sheltering the boy, even though he committed an offence. I have stopped beating him, because the neighbours said that this is not done in this country, and was ashamed of behaving differently from others. I really don't know what to do with my boy.''

For children the new situation has become significant because they cannot get the support and security they need from their parents at a time when this is most essential to them. Let us consider, for instance, the position of a child in school. He often may find it difficult to keep pace with the ordinary curriculum, particularly when subjects to be studied are related to abstract thinking. He cannot get the necessary help from his parents at home because they themselves lack knowledge in these affairs. As a result many children drift away from elementary school. It is only in recent years that the Ministry of Education has taken real steps to provide appropriate material in school with the aim to prevent a large number of children from dropping out of school. The result would be that children who have no basic elementary education and who have not been trained in systematic thinking and learning will not be able to acquire a skilled job and often not even semi-skilled work. This may have negative repercussions on their future behavior and on their smooth integration into a sophisticated society, which is ruled by science and technology.

In this connection it should be stressed that the interests and needs of children necessitate their conforming to normative behavior of the new environment. They are instinctly drawn to it, for they feel that this is the key to their future. Apart from this, there exists a strong desire to be accepted, to become equal, and to be regarded on the same footing as their play-mates. On this issue there has also developed a clash of interests between the old traditional values which the family was concerned to uphold and the pressures and tendencies in the new society. Children want to establish and to foster new relationships, which belong mostly outside the family circle, while parents try to prevent such relations *because* they are outside the family circle. Thus the basis for conflicts has been widened, and has often been the cause for family conflicts and disruptions.

In the Juvenile Court in Tel-Aviv a girl, aged 16 years was charged with having committed a theft. Prior to disposing of the case I discussed with her this matter and the ensuing consequences should it happen again. She said, among other things the following: "You can be sure that I won't steal any more. I am already engaged, and soon I must be getting married." I asked her why she "must" get married and she replied: "My father promised him that I'll agree to marry him. I can't do a thing about it because my father gave him his word of honor. It is against my own wish, but I have to obey. It is not like with you Europeans. If my father promises something for me, I have to do it as if I myself had promised it. With you Europeans it is different, and you are much better off." This girl, illiterate as she was, expressed a serious conflict of which she had become aware. She had come to feel and to understand emotionally the deficiencies of the old traditional way, but she saw the advantages, as they seemed to her, which are inherent in the new environment.

It is not unusual to hear parents complain in the Juvenile Court that the new conditions, the influence of the new environment, and the hitherto unknown habits and customs are to blame for the delinquent behavior of their children. Some admit their inability to take care of their children in a more appropriate way, and they request the judge to find a suitable solution. Others mention the same reasons but try to protect and shelter their children. Many parents regard it as a great shame on their family to have come to court. Some feel that they have failed, and this determines their attitude towards the Juvenile Court and towards society at large.

The following case may illustrate a situation which frequently arises in juvenile courts in Israel. Two boys aged 12 were charged with having stolen some scrap iron. Both appeared in court with their fathers and both denied having committed the offence. I explained to the boys that I would adjourn the case to enable the prosecuting officer to bring evidence on this matter. One of the fathers interjected saying that his son had nothing to do with the whole matter. Then, two witnesses gave evidence that made it clear that they had stolen the scrap iron. The father who had first interjected approached me near the bench and said in a whisper: "You must understand I was teacher to Jewish children in Persia for over 30 years. I taught them to lead an honest life and obey the commandments. And now how is it possible that here in Israel my own son should become a thief? I cannot admit this. I keep an eye on him all day long, I don't allow him to play in the streets because I think it is no good for his upbringing. If he really should have committed this crime, I could not tolerate the shame he would bring upon my whole family." It became imperative to help the boy regain acceptance within his family and to assist his father in accepting the reality of the situation. I placed the boy on probation because it seemed necessary to help him reorient himself with the help of the probation officer, to alley existing anxieties of his parents, and to soften rigid attitudes.

Reactions of the different oriental communities to the impact of Western culture is not necessarily a uniform one. These communities have no homogeneous background and tradition, and we witness different reactions if they are exposed to same conflict situations. This is particularly the case in relation to the family while being confronted with problems arising out of the way of life in a rapidly changing society like that of Israel. We have observed another important phenomena, namely, juvenile delinquency among newcomers usually becomes manifest several years after their arrival in Israel. The following reasons may account for this. During the first few years after immigration, the child feels insecure in the new environment and his inhibitions operate to avoid it as much a possible. It takes time for the influence of the new environment to penetrate the family structure. It also takes time for identity conflicts to reach a point at which they disrupt the family unit. If these things happen rapidly, juvenile delinquency is likely to result. In addition, as time passes, failures and frustrations increase, and in many instances they result in maladjustment and in other forms of negative behaviour.

If we turn now to review briefly the situation among Israeli Arabs, one is confronted with similar situations as is the case with Jewish people originating from the Oriental countries. The family structure of Arabs has been the stronghold of the patriarchal system, and this system is being shaken to its roots. During the period between the two world wars, and with dramatic effect since the establishment of Israel, new ideas and ways of life have begun to penetrate this system. For 30 years Israeli Arabs have been living and have taken part—actively or passively—in a dynamic society, in which Jews with modern Western ideas provided the leadership and constituted the majority of the population. There have been great transformations within the Arab economic structure in Israel. Agriculture is no longer the most important source of income and is therefore no longer the most common occupation. A considerable number are employed in the Jewish labor market, which has opened up for them hitherto unknown opportunities. As a result of these developments, a considerable number of young people from rural areas now acquire new professions or are employed in new jobs. They work away from their villages, although many may continue to live there. The mere fact that a large number of village people no longer till their own land but now work in other places and at other occupations has had a major impact on village life. Many of the functions which traditionally belonged to men were of necessity transferred to the shoulders of women, this in itself constitutes a great change with consequences for the family unit.

All social services which are available to Jews in Israel—education, health care, welfare, national insurance, and so on—are also available to Arab citizens. The standard of living among both urban and rural Israeli Arabs is much higher than that of citizens in surrounding Arab countries. Children are aware of the changes which have impact on all spheres of life.

CHILD WELFARE LAWS

In this section a brief description is given of several laws that deal with the protection of children and young persons. These laws have direct bearing, in one way or another, on general matters of child welfare. The laws are discussed in the order in which they were passed by the Knesset (Israeli Parliament).

EDUCATION

Until the establishment of the State of Israel in 1948, there was no compulsory elementary education in this country. It was therefore natural that the Knesset was most eager to introduce a law to this effect as soon as possible. By the Compulsory Education Law of 1949 any "child" aged five to 13 years inclusive is obliged to attend a recognized shcool, and by doing so he is entitled to education free of charge. Furthermore, "young person," those aged 14 to 17 years inclusive, who, for some reason or another, have not finished all grades of elementary school, must fulfill the prescribed eight grades in special schools, mostly evening schools. A most important amendment, passed on July 2, 1969, raised the age of compulsory school attendance to 15 years. Furthermore, the whole system of elementary and secondary education has been remodeled along new lines. There will be, as it were, three distinct groups, two of them on the level of free and compulsory education. Schooling for the third age group, those age 16 to 17, is geared to continuing higher education. It is not compulsory, nor is it free. There are, however, financial grants to enable gifted pupils to continue at a secondary school level. It is hoped that this new system will more effectively reconcile the needs of the child and the demands of a technological society.

Although elementary education is firmly established by now, there are still many children who do not finish the grades prescribed by law. This problem is of paramount importance in a heterogenous society like that of Israel. The chronological development in Israel increasingly requires general knowledge of a rather high nature, particularly specific knowledge is in growing demand. Even jobs of a simple or semiskilled nature now require at least ten years of school education. However, raising the age level at which a child can leave school will not, per se, provide an incentive to attend school for those who encounter, for various reasons, difficulties by remaining in school. A genuine implementation of compulsory education has to pay special attention to the lower grades of the elementary school system, otherwise it may widen rather than narrow the educational gap. It is superfluous to stress that provision by law for better and higher education does not necessarily imply that larger groups of people will be able to benefit from it. Something else must be done to achieve that goal.

CHILD MARRIAGE

It was customary among certain sections of the local population, particularly among those originating from Moselm countries—Jews and Arabs alike—to marry off girls at a tender age. Not infrequently one encountered young women and mothers, as young as 14 or 15 years old, who were attending to their household and to their children, instead of attending elementary or secondary schools. This custom developed over the centuries as an important barrier to immorality (and was combined with strong taboos concerning social intercourse between young males and females outside the family circle). Girls were thereby protected from temptation, as it were, and thus the social status of the family was not imperiled.

In the Juvenile Court mothers would sometimes explain their inability to take proper care of their children on the ground that they were children themselves when they were married. This fact has been a source of great grievance for many, although they became conscious of the problem only in Israel where they encountered quite different customs.

Such a situation occured recently in the juvenile court in Tel-Aviv. The mother of a 15-year-old boy, who was charged with several serious offences, said that she was unable to control her boy. It was evident that she had taken no interest in him, nor in her other two children. It was also evident that she was very afraid of him. The report submitted by the probation officer mentioned that this mother was born in Persia and had been married off at the age of 12 years to a man ten years older than she. He had been married before but had no children. When she was 14 years old, he divorced the mother because she did not become pregnant. The mother remarried at the age of 20. She has no affection towards the three children of this marriage, and all of them have come to need special care.

Child marriage was so frequent that one of the first laws in Israel in the field of child welfare was concerned with its abolition. By the Marriage Age Law of 1950 no girl under 17 years was allowed to marry. The law provides for sanctions for a person who marries a girl under this age, for the parent or guardian who gives his consent, and for the person who performs the marriage ceremony. By special application, however, a district court judge may give consent to marry at an earlier age if reasons are given. If a marriage is performed below the age prescribed by the law, the marriage can be nullified, if application is made to the court when the girl concerned is still under 19 years. This covers instances in which the marriage was performed outside Israel. It can be said that this law is not generally accepted, although at first it encountered objections in various quarters.

CHILD LABOR

Just as child marriage was a custom in this part of the world, so was child labor. It can be assumed that this fact prompted the British Mandatory Government to introduce, in 1945, legislation to regulate, to a certain extent, the employment of children. The regulation was, however, of short duration. The Knesset replaced it with two laws which are to a certain extent complementary, the Youth Labour Law and the Apprenticeship Law. It is no accident that these two laws were discussed and passed by the Knesset at practically the same time.

The Youth Labour Law of 1953 defines a "child" as a person below 16 years, and an "adolescent" as a person between 16 and 17 inclusive. According to this law, a child who has not attained the age of 14 years shall not be employed in any kind of work, save for itinerent trading but only if he has a special permit for such trading. Employment is prohibited for children below the age of 16 years in places such as hotels or dance halls, in places where mentally sick persons are treated or other places which may have a detrimental effect on the well-being of a child or a young person. The law also provides for appropriate medical examinations, for regulation of working hours, for vocational guidance, rest hours, and yearly vacations.

Penalties are provided for in case of contraventions. The Youth Labour Law has gained wide recognition, and practically all factories and organized workshops adhere to it, but it is less observed in small workshops, run by one or two persons. The fact is that many young children drop out of elementary school and look for employment in just such small places and small workshops, hoping not to be caught there by the law. Theirs is usually not regular work. They float from one job to another, and their salaries are naturally not in accordance with regulations. This group includes a rather large number of errand boys, who are usually of a tender age. Matters in this field have become more problematic and complicated because raising the age at which a child could leave school is accompanied by a raising of the working age.

The Apprenticeship Law of 1953 defines a "juvenile" as a person who has not yet reached the age of 18. (An "apprentice" is a juvenile who works in order to acquire a trade by guided practical work and by attending approved trade lessons within the meaning of the law.) The law makes provision for the length of time and the curriculum of the apprenticeship period, for wages, examinations, vacations, number of apprentices who may be employed at a certain place, and the qualifications and duties of employers. There is a legal provision for the appointment of a trade apprenticeship board with an elaboration of its duties, and provision for supervisors and inspectors. The law carries penalties, and has proved effective for the welfare of those young people who come under its purview.

PROTECTION OF CHILDREN IN A SEXUAL ASSAULT

An amendment to the law of evidence was enacted by the Knesset in 1955. This amendment deals with the protection of children under the age of 14 who have been involved in a sexual assault. Under this law provision is made that youth interrogators are appointed to interrogate children on the commission of such offence, and children are exempted from giving evidence in court, save with the permission of a youth interrogator. Until this special law came into effect, no statutes concerning children who were involved in such offences were available in Israel. One could therefore do very little to help children who were in need of it.

Three categories of children are protected by this law: those who committed a sex offence, those who witness a sex offence, and victims of a sexual offence. In this paper only this last group will be discussed.

Apprehending sex offenders is greatly hindered because the victims are often ashamed to lodge a complaint about this type of offence. It is also commonplace that offenders threaten children with vengeance should they disclose what happened. These threats are taken seriously by children, and they add to the secrecy which surrounds sex offences. Furthermore, even parents prefer to conceal the fact that their child has become a victim of a sex offence, lest they may be blamed for negligence of their child. Thus we can see in many instances the interesting feature of a shared secrecy between the victim and the offender.

Experience has shown that children react differently when they are sexually assaulted. This may depend on their personality, on their age, on the atmosphere prevailing at home, on their relations with their parents, and on the circumstances of the commission of the offence. There are children who do seem not disturbed: others have strong guilt feelings. Some are ashamed of what happened to them, others have a tendency to tell their friends freely about it and try to show off. Some kind of provocations or half-innocent remarks sometimes play a role in causing the offence. Often children become involved in sexual play out of curiosity or are dragged into it accidentally. Invariably, emotional upheaval could be observed in those instances when force was used while committing the sexual offence.

Naturally, the child victim is himself the most important person to provide information which may lead to the apprehension of the offender and to his subsequent trial. The victims are, however, of tender age, and, at the police interrogation, or while giving evidence in court, are unable to relate coherently the facts which surrounded the commission of the offence. This may depend directly on the circumstances of the sexual assault, but it may also be the result of the personality make-up of a particular child.

Prosecuting authorities base their case first of all on information from the child who was the victim, and therefore they are called upon to relate as many details as possible. For many children this may mean reliving an experience that was most unpleasant and traumatic. They may therefore have difficulties in going through the experience again, and "blocking," "forgetting," and "giving false descriptions" of it. Thus the information of the child victim may be of no great help, and the apprehended sex offender may be acquitted instead of convicted.

By the law of 1955 youth interrogators are appointed to investigate children who were involved in a sexual offence, and to give evidence in court instead of the child. Those interrogators are experts in interviewing techniques and mental hygiene. It is felt that an appropriate expert approach at the initial stage of the interrogation may diminish or even obliterate the trauma caused to a child who has been a victim to a sexual offence. The first contact with the child while he is relating the story of what happened is of vital importance to the child concerned. This is often also the case in a court hearing. Our experience has shown that youth interrogators are capable of getting much more information from the victims than even the most experienced policeman. Contrary to the latter's approach, which is directed by his habitual manner of interrogating delinquents, the success of the youth interrogator's method depends on an approach of understanding and special attention. This professional and understanding manner may open the heart of the child and may thus make it possible and even convenient, for him to talk. At the same time that the expert's contact with the victim diminishes the traumatic effects of the experience, important and relevant information is extracted.

The following case would best illustrate this point. A youth interrogator went to the home of a nine-year-old girl whose parents had complained that a sex offence had been committed on her. At that point the child was completely unable to talk. At the second visit to the home which took place the following day, she was still very timid, and the youth interrogator realized that the child would not be able to disclose the necessary information in a direct manner. She therefore asked the child what the dwelling of the man looked like. After some hesitation, the girl took a sheet of paper and pencil, drew a room and a roof, and then, while still drawing, explained a bit more freely: "Here is a table with three chairs. Above it is a lampshade, and there, in the corner, is a bed. Here was the man, and I was standing there. Suddenly he drew me up to the bed, and I don't know what happened next." After having recounted this, the girl looked anxious and waited silently, as if wondering what the youth interrogator's reaction would be. She was extremely relieved when the woman continued to talk to her in the same normal way as before, without, for instance, putting to the child the question of why she had gone to the room in the first place. The child, being reassured by the behavior of the youth interrogator, was then able to talk further and to reveal all the important details in this case. At the end of the interview she could even express the fear that she herself was to blame because she agreed to go with the man to his room. It was evident that the talk with the youth interrogator relieved her of her guilt feelings.

When an offender is apprehended and taken to court, he may take advantage of a child's fear to relate the whole story in his presence, or he may cast doubts on the victim's story by involving him in contradictions. Indeed, experience has shown that it is very easy to bring a child to express a conflicting story while giving evidence in court. As a consequence, the child may be further victimized and may be considered a liar because he does not know how to comply with legal procedure and therefore yields to confusing questions put to him. In this respect, the defendant or the defending counsel, may be instrumental in enhancing the possible traumatic effect of the child victim. The Knesset has therefore entrusted the matter of evidence to the youth interrogators. It is the particular interrogator who has taken down the details from a child victim, who gives evidence in court on behalf of the child, or who can permit the child to give evidence himself. In a survey which I made on 1,697 child victims it was indicated that permission to testify in court was granted to 14 percent of child victims over the age of ten and to 8 percent under ten. In these instances, evidence was given in the presence of the youth interrogator who investigated the case. His presence during court proceedings is of vital importance to the child victim and to court hearings as well. To ensure the legal status of the youth interrogator in court when he permitted a child victim to give evidence himself, an amendment was passed in 1962, according to which evidence of the child victim may be discontinued if the youth interrogator is of the opinion that continuance of the testimony may cause mental harm to the child. Experience has shown that while giving evidence in court, some children who were thought able to stand in the witness box became panicky, showed symptoms of bewilderment, and fell into the mental state the law had intended to prevent. The decision to discontinue this testimony rests with the court. The youth interrogator can also be of assistance in the field of prevention. He has been trained to understand and evaluate mental and social conditions. If circumstances require he can take immediate steps to transfer to the appropriate authorities those cases in need of special care.

It is maintained that this new law is a unique venture whereby elementary legal rights of defendants have been combined with a method of protecting children who have been victims of sexual assault. Experience has shown that since this law has come into effect in 1955, more people have reported such offences to the authorities instead of trying to conceal them, because they are aware of the protection of their child. We maintain that this law is in the interests of child victims and of society at large.

ADOPTION OF CHILDREN

The Adoption of Children law came into force in 1966. Until then, adoption of children proceeded according to provisions laid down in rules. The competence to make an adoption order is vested with the District court. Before we elaborate on the application and implementation of this new law, it is relevant to comment on the welfare of the children on whose behalf the court is requested to intervene. Invariably, when infants or children of a tender age are brought to the juvenile court because they were abandoned or criminally neglected by their parents, or because the infant was an illegitmate child living under inadequate conditions, or was living with a mother who practiced prostitution, the question has arisen whether the interests of the child concerned would not require an adoption order rather than an order of care and protection. An adoption order is more or less a final act of placing the child with new parents, and it is just this finality on which the welfare of the child and his future development may depend. However, in cases of care and protection the smooth and normal development of the child may be jeopardized by the unwarranted interference of parents, and also by repeated placements of the growing child. Even so, a child may have to be placed a number of times. This may be because of lack of placement facilities or the difficulties of a particular child, and applies as well to childrens' homes, even if run on a small scale. Foster families are sometimes put under heavy pressure by the parents for whose children they are caring. This eventually may prevent them from continuing to fulfill their duty.

It is interesting to note that there exists great resentment, on the part of individuals as well as society at large, if an adoption is made without consent of the natural parent. Legal procedures in adoption cases are much more stringent when it comes to removing a child from his parents than in cases of care and protection. The decisive and basic difference lies in the matter of dispossesion. The Knesset has accepted that basic difference, but has also made provision for issuing an adoption order even without consent of parents. Among the many important provisions of the adoption of children law, two sections are concerned with consent by the natural parent. Section 8 states that the court shall not make an adoption order without such consent. The limitations of this section are set off, however, by section 11 which states:

A court may make an adoption order even without the consent of a parent where any of the following has been proved to its satisfaction.
(1) The parent has abandoned the adoptee or has constantly failed to fulfill his duty towards him.
(2) The parent is unable to express his opinion or there is no reasonable possibility of ascertaining his opinion.
(3) The parent's refusal to consent to the adoption is determined by immoral motives or an unlawful purpose.

In a recent decision in the Haifa District Court an adoption order was issued although the natural father of the adoptee objected and refused to give his consent. In his reasons for this order the judge pointed out that the natural father had not shown any interest in his child for the past 12 years, and had not looked after the material and emotional well-being of his child. In contrast, the potential adopter had looked after the child and had cared for him. In addition, the child himself preferred the potential adopter who had taken care of him all those years. The same court has made similar decision before, undoubtedly in the interest of the child.

Provisions are made in this law so that an adoption order can be made in the case of a person below the age of 18 years. A single person or a person who is not at least 18 years older than the person to be adopted cannot adopt. A probationary period of at least six months is required before the final order is granted. The court may appoint, even if not requested to do so, a guardian for an adoptee. And last but not least, a court shall not make an adoption order under this law unless it has received beforehand a written report by a welfare officer. The Adoption of Children law also makes provision that no adoption order can be issued save by ensuring that the potential adopter adheres to the same religious faith as the adoptee. Also, in instances in which the adoptee understands the matter of adoption, such an order can only be made after ascertaining that the adoptee agrees to be adopted by the potential adopter.

Sanctions are provided for in instances in which somebody publishes, without permission of the court, any details pertaining to the identification of the potential adopter, an adoptee or his parent, and those who filed the application in court for an adoption order. Sanctions are provided for those who offer money or other benefits, or who accept those without permission of the court. Court proceedings are not open to the public.

CHILDREN IN NEED

Another law concerning the welfare of children was passed by the Knesset in 1960, namely the Youth Law (Care and Supervision). Under this law social workers are appointed by special proclamation, to apply to the juvenile court when judicial intervention on behalf of a minor is required. Application to the juvenile court can be made if there is no responsible person to take care of the minor or if the person responsible for the minor is unable to take proper care of him or to supervise him, or he neglects to do so. Application also can be made if the minor has committed an act which is a criminal offence but he has not been brought to trial for this offence, or if the minor is vagrant, begging alms or hawking goods. It can be made if the child is under bad influences, or lives in a place which is permanently used for some criminal purpose, and if the minor's physical or spiritual well-being is affected. Another cause was added by the Knesset in 1974 whereby intervention can also be initiated on the ground that the child is being battered. According to this amendment various professional people who deal with children should inform the social worker whenever they suspect child abuse. Application to the juvenile court can be made on behalf of any minor under 18 years. Court decision, however, become void when the minor reaches the age of 18.

The juvenile court, while adjudicating a minor who is in need of care and supervision, applies proceedings which are civil by nature and therefore different from criminal proceedings. The scope of the inquiry is much wider than it is for criminal cases and much evidence may therefore be admissible that would be ruled out as irrelevent in a criminal case. Since the court is investigating the conduct of the child and his parents, it can hear evidence of past conduct. Both parents and child are compellable to give evidence although neither of them can be compelled to incriminate himself. The result of these differences, is, among others, that the juvenile court may often be able to intervene to protect a minor when, owing to deficiency of legal evidence, it would be helpless to take care of him. In Israel, special rules were published to this effect. There have also been decision by the Supreme Court which recognized the wide range of proceedings in implementing this law.

Under this law a social worker, who has been appointed for that purpose, may enter private houses in case of emergency and remove a minor even without a court order for a period up to seven days, during which time the case must be brought to court. Enforcement of court orders, except for special cases, and supervision of children placed under court order is also the duty of the social worker.

Any court order under this law can be made for a period of not more than three years. If a request is made for a renewal of the order, the court has to be satisfied that the same conditions exist as at the time when the original order was made.

Decisions by the court can be altered, amended, or rescinded at a court hearing, upon the written request of the social worker, the minor himself, or his parents or the person responsible for him. The court itself makes the decision according to the material brought forward. In all decisions the court has to give its reasons in writing, as any decisions by courts has to be made in writing.

Application by the social worker for court intervention is by way of being a last resort. This is done only when there exists opposition—on the part of the minor, or his parent or guardian—to the suggestions made by the welfare agency. But once the matter is referred to the social worker in order to secure court intervention, many parents and sometimes even minors are at this stage inclined to accept or at least to consider those suggestions which were previously made by the welfare agency. Such a change in attitude is prompted by a desire to avoid court intervention. It means, in fact, that the court plays an important role in a kind of motivation and perhaps socialization process which occurs. In those instances it is obvious that shame, fear, social stigma, and the like account for such change in attitude.

It can safely be assumed that those children who were referred for court intervention represent only a fraction of those who were in fact in need of care. The small figure can be explained on the following grounds. First, there is not sufficient understanding of the extent to which the court situation can motivate changes in the attitude of parents and minors alike. Second, many local authorities have not yet implemented this law, because it would involve them in additional financial burdens. They maintain therefore that the central government should be responsible for implementation. Third, application for court intervention results in most instances in the removal of the child to an education establishment which families wish to avoid. It has been our experience in Israel that minors who are dealt with by the juvenile court because they are in need of care and supervision are more often placed away from their home in comparison to juvenile offenders. Children of the latter group are frequently left with their parents either under supervision of a probation officer, or of a social worker or without supervision altogether. This can seldom be done with children who are in need of care and supervision. Their parents are either unable to exercise control over them, or they are themselves in need of control because they neglect their children. Frequently, the only way of protecting their children is to remove them to better and healthier surroundings.

The likelihood that children also will be removed from their homes is greater if they are at a tender age, because they need elementary physical care, more than older children do, which is more easily observable than emotional deprivation. Yet, as I have pointed out, placements at a tender age necessitate in most instances repeated placements. These, in the end, may defeat the initial purpose of care and supervision. Many a minor is thus liable to become a problem child. It is an interesting reflection on the problems involved in these cases that 95 percent of minors who were brought to court had to be placed away from their parents, either at an educational institution or with foster parents, or in infant or baby homes. The primary factor is the removal from their parents, and it is of secondary importance to which place they are removed, although this is of course per se an important issue. A different picture presents itself in cases of juvenile offenders. Here, only 10 percent have to be removed from their own home, to which they normally return after a period of two to three years.

Apart from placement orders our law makes provision for a number of treatment facilities if the minor is permitted to stay with his parents. He is allowed to stay after he or his parent has received directions as to their respective behavior, or to pledge to adhere to directions given to them. Otherwise the court may appoint a counsellor to guide and supervise a minor (which can be done only with the consent of counsellor) or place the minor under the supervision of the social worker who applied for the intervention of the juvenile court.

Whatever decision is made by the court, a minor and his parent must be given a chance to voice the suggestions they themselves may have to change the conditions which have led to court intervention. It does therefore happen that in view of their remarks that the court may postpone making a final decision pending improvement of the situation. It is in these instances that the court is becoming involved in a treatment situation. Longstanding grievances and misunderstandings can thus be aired in court, each party given credit and understanding on the merit of each case. We have found that after such clarifications decisions by the court were more readily accepted and have sometimes become a means to further child-parent contact. Of course, such a procedure can be envisaged for minors who are able, even on a small intellectual level, to communicate at least some of the problems which bother them.

It is noteworthy that this law makes no provision to take punitive actions against parents or guardians, even if they are the source for the neglect of the particular minor. It means that this law is clearly confined to look after the welfare of minors who are in need of care and supervision. Parents, however, may be ordered by court to contribute to the maintenance of their child, completely or partly, or to treatment expenses. This can only be done after clarification of their economic condition.

JUVENILE DELINQUENCY

As we probably all know, juvenile delinquency has been increasing in many countries over the last three decades or so. Numerous factors account for this, such as upheavals following changes because of immigration and migration, the changing status of fathers and mothers within the family, rapid economic development and industrialization, the enormous growth of cities, the change of attitude to religious values, the impact of mass media such as radio and television, and so on. Particularly three factors contribute to juvenile delinquency in Israel. These are the break-up of the family unit, the clash of cultures in a melting-pot setting, and the rapid development of a technological society. Each of these factors alone is of sufficient magnitude to create situations which can lead to delinquent behaviour. Many individuals, however, must deal with all three simultaneously. There are also, of course, emotional factors which may result in delinquency. Our experience over many years has shown, however, that emotional disturbances by themselves are seldom the determining issue but rather a by-product of the factors mentioned above.

As far as the types of offences committed by juveniles in Israel are concerned, serious crimes are infrequent. There are almost no cases of robbery, murder, arson or extortion. Rape is virtually nonexistent, and even minor sex offences occur on a small scale. All these offences can be regarded as violent delinquent patterns. Of all offences committed which were dealt with by juvenile courts over the last ten years, offences against property amounted to 82.8 percent.

Large numbers of children and young people in Israel often find themselves facing a sequence of frustrating situations. For instance, many children who belong to oriental Jewish communities find it difficult to keep pace with the ordinary school curriculum, although they are not mentally retarded. Many eventually drift away from school without finishing the prescribed grades in elementary school. They early become aware, albeit not intellectually, that their failure to finish school hampers their integration into Israel society and their ultimate failure. Many of them hold a grudge against the school which, as they see it, prevented them from gaining the social status of their peers.

The public continues to be alarmed, and many think that something drastic should be done to curb it. However, there is a discrepancy between public impressions and actual facts. Actually, there is an increase in serious criminal behavior by adults, but the public usually does not differentiate between juvenile offenders who are tried in the juvenile court and adults, including young adults, who are tried in courts for adults. What goes on in adult courts usually receives wide publicity via newspaper reports, and reporting is not accurate to such extent as to distinguish between juvenile offenses and those of adults. The real problem concerning juvenile delinquents is the large number of recidivists. Although recidivism can, to a certain extent be attributed to personal factors, the high percentage of recidivists in all age groups points to insufficient and inadequate special community services. To prevent juvenile delinquent behavior, Israel has established a system, whereby preventive action is taken for youngsters aged 12 to 17 years. Sheltered workshops have been established for those who have not finished an elementary school education. It was foreseen that they would encounter great difficulties in adjusting themselves to regular working hours, and usually they would also find it hard to get used to permanent jobs. Rehabilitation centers were put up all over the country and had no detrimental effect on their status. In these centers they are taught elementary school subjects, and at the same time they are taught various vocations such as carpentry, shoemaking, blacksmithery and gardening and for girls, sewing, weaving, and embroidery. Special methods are used which aim, among other things, to create personal pride in accomplishment in a particular field. An endeavour is made to rid the atmosphere of the negative competitive aspects in a learning process in which the children failed previously, and which may have been a contributing factor in their general maladjustment.

JUVENILE COURTS

It is my contention that the juvenile court presents, by its very nature, a dynamic situation which entails inherently different individual reactions, and in which intrafamily situations and conflicts can be expressed. One is confronted there with crises and stress situations, with failures of children and parents, and, in many instances, with inadequate community resources. A most important characteristic of the juvenile court is that it concerns young people who are still in the process of growing, mentally and physically, and who are in many respects dependent on others. Furthermore, while adjudicating a juvenile offender, the court concerns also the situation of parents, siblings and friends, the condition of the neighborhood, and so forth. These factors have to be taken into account while trying to understand the motivation behind an offense. They have to be considered again prior to making a decision on how to dispose of the case. In other words, while using such approach, the juvenile court can make a contribution in the field of treatment and prevention alike. The following may illustrate such a situation. A 15-year-old girl was brought to the juvenile court by a policeman; she came with her father. She was suspected of having stolen genuine diamonds, worth many thousands of pounds. On the matter itself she told me that she was going with her girl friends to a party, and on the spur of the moment she took the diamonds from the place where she was working. In court one could feel that there was great tension between Rachel and her father. While I was trying to soften the aggressive outbreaks on both sides, Rachel said: "You can see how my parents behave and how they react. It is their fault that I am here in court. They think that a girl who does not always stay at home is leading a loose life. They don't want to get used to customs in the country. Life here is different from what it was in Egypt. They refuse to accept this, and they lock themselves in their home and want me to do the same." The father said in part, "We give her all what we have, and she doesn't need to go to work. She meets all sorts of people whom we don't know, and we also don't know their parents. She keeps company with people strange to us, and this is a big blot on the honor of our family. We tell her that she has

82

to keep the traditions in our family, but she won't listen to us. We can't understand how children behave in this country. This cannot be good for Israel.'' Here I was confronted with a real crisis situation, which had been going on for some time, but which broke out clearly in the court, the social institution which is regarded in the peoples' minds as a punitive setting. The girl and her father, both expressed their conflict, reflected in their opposed positions. Both turned to the judge as an arbiter, as it were, who should decide the issue. But the situations indicated also that the girl spoke out of fear of punishment, and the father expected exactly to do this, to punish the girl after he had failed in his endeavours to change her behavior.

I have observed that great importance is attached to the attitude which the court is taking on a particular issue. If the court can be tolerant of the misdeeds of children, many parents can then ''afford''as it were, to be tolerant as well. The negative impression which the court might have had on parents is thus diminished, which in turn may lead to a better intra-family communication. I found it advisable to adjourn the young girl's case in order to find out whether or not a change in the behavior of both parties could take place. I was quite convinced that, if at all, this could be brought about only by using the court as a mediator. The general presumption that swift justice is good justice does not necessarily apply to the juvenile court. In this setting an adjournment to finish a case is often advisable as part of the process of rehabilitation. It should naturally be made use of selectively, overriding sometimes the demand for ''efficiency.'' I found it therefore expedient to introduce at this point the probation officer, asking him to be in touch with this family in order to iron out existing conflict situations. I adjourned the case three more times, each time having a full conversation in court with all parties concerned. I have made use of this technique because it has been my experience that by the mere fact that the trial is still undecided while talks between members of the family and the probation officer are going on, many a family can mobilize potential forces to bridge differences. Eventually Rachel was put on probation so that the situation which was established in the court setting could effectively be continued outside it.

Another item needs to be remarked upon. It also belongs in the domain of a judge in the juvenile court that he should be well acquainted with existing community facilities for juvenile offenders and that he should know how to make use of them. He need not, of course, be an expert on different treatment and correction methods for juvenile offenders, but he should possess knowledge of the process of their implementation, and also of their limitations. Otherwise it may happen that adequate diagnostic treatment, and correctional resources are available which a judge may fail to make use of, or which he does not use in an appropriate way. His alertness of special needs are also essential.

In 1971 a new Juvenile Court Law was enacted which deals with trial, punishment, and modes of treatment of juvenile offenders. Two courts now have jurisdiction over juvenile offenders; the Magistrates' Juvenile Court and the District Juvenile Court. The latter court deals with very serious offences, which require trial by three judges, and also serves as a court of appeal. The Magistrates' Juvenile Court is empowered to try minors for felonies under the section specified in the order. Another section of the law states that, save with the consent of the attorney-general, a minor shall not be brought to trial for an offence if a year has passed since its commission. The significant aspect involved is that, the police should deal efficiently with matters of interrogation so that trial can take place without further delay. It is of interest to note that the Knesset displayed an ambivalent attitude towards parents. On the one hand, a court can decide, prior to hearing the case, that a parent should not be present at a court hearing. This can be done, however, only for special reasons. On the other hand, the Knesset established that parents may file any application in court instead of the minor, and they may also examine witnesses and have arguments heard instead of the minor or together with him. This section is of particular importance if looked at from the point of improving parent-child relationships.

BIBLIOGRAPHY

Reifen, D. *The Juvenile Court in Israel,* (Jerusalem: Ministry of Justice, 1964).

———, *The Magistrate and the Welfare Worker* (Milan: Centro Nazionale Difesa Sociale, 1962).

———, "New Ventures of Law Enforcement in Israel," *Journal of Criminal, Law, Criminology and Police Science*, Vol. 58 (March, 1967).

———, "Observations on the Juvenile Court in Israel" (Jerusalem, 1965). *Prevention of Crime and the Treatment of Offenders in Israel* Report to the Third U.N. Congress on the Prevention of Crime and the Treatment of Offenders.

———, "Sex Offences and the Protection of Children," *'The Canadian Journal of Corrections,* Vol. 8 (April, 1966).

———, *The Juvenile Court in a Changing Society,* (Philadelphia: University of Pennsylvania Press, 1972).

Shoham, S. Giora *The Myth of Tantalus* (Queensland: University of Queensland Press 1979).

———*The Mark of Cain* (Jerusalem: Israel University Press, 1970).

Shichor, S. and Kirschenbaum, A. "Juvenile Delinquency and New Towns: the Case for Israel" *Youth Crime and Juvenile Justice: International Perspectives* (P. Friday and V.L. Stewart (eds.) New York: Praeger, 1977).

6

Netherlands

Josine Junger-Tas

Dr. Junger-Tas makes an objective analysis of the Dutch
system of child care and protection and provides a comprehensive description of services designed to meet the needs of
troubled children. She shows the importance of a sensitized
school system which recognizes trouble early and moves
quickly from theory to practice. She describes the Dutch
programs to deal with learning problems associated with
dyslexia and other handicaps. Recognition of the basic needs
and rights of all children in the total national plan is seen in
a very complete description of governmental and private
services. The Dutch policy obviously is for early recognition
of trouble and definitive action without delay. Of special interest is the concept of "reading mothers" who find their
places in the school along with the teacher working as a
team on behalf of their children.

Editor

INTRODUCTION

In this report I will try to present an objective view of the
Dutch system of child care and protection, which means that I
will review some of the problems our country faces in the field of

child care as well as in the struggle to control juvenile delinquency. I will take this more critical approach because I think this will be of more value to the reader than would be a too flattering picture of our extended and well-known system of child protection. The reason for this is that many of our problems are by no means unique but are shared by most of the so-called highly developed and technically advanced societies. So it would seem rather useless—in a book like this—to enumerate all our successful institutions and praise their excellent functioning.

It will be much more worthwhile to explain some of the mistakes we made, and to indicate some of the solutions to pressing problems we are now experimenting with. It is my hope that both will stimulate the reader and make him reflect on the different possibilities of social change, in order to promote a healthier social environment that will create happier children.

SOME BASIC DATA

It will be useful in order to understand the working of the Dutch system of child care and protection, to give some background information on its essentials. To start with, the Netherlands presently have a population of about 13 million inhabitants, most of whom are concentrated in the western urban areas. This includes about 4.5 million of children below the age of 18 years. In the sixties a total of about 45,000 minors were handled by the child care and protection system, which is about 1 percent of our juvenile population. Since 1960 the total population of minors has not much changed in terms of number. But the population of minors under child care and protection has dropped dramatically. The number of children within the child protection system has been falling from 42,181 in 1960 to 24,241 in 1976.[1] As there are no signs that deviant and delinquent behavior among juveniles have diminished, policy in this respect must have changed and other ways must have been adopted to handle youngsters in trouble. For one thing, placement in an institution (including private institutions and homes) is becoming less frequent. Judicial authorities seem to prefer to place a child in a foster family or to let him stay in his own family. This trend is a clear one and it still goes on. Parallel to this evolution, length of stay in the institutions has been reduced: from 1972 to 1976 the average length of stay in institutions for normal children has been reduced from 16.5 to 14.4 months, and in treatment institutions from 20.0 months to 16.1 months, both significant reductions. However this change in policy does not touch all categories of children, that go through the juvenile system, to the same extent.

We can distinguish three categories of children. The first includes *children under guardianship* whose parents are deprived of their parental rights (in 1976: ± 12,000) The second group is composed of *children under supervision* of a family guardian are those who are "threatened with moral or physical danger" (1976: ± 12,000). The third is *juvenile offenders*, who have been found guilty of a criminal offense (1976: ± 6,000). The first two categories include children in need of care and protection, the third category covers adjudicated delinquents. The proportion of supervised children placed in an institution did not change from 1967 to 1976. Although the absolute number of children placed under supervision declined by ± 12,000 during that period, the proportion of these children placed in institutions remained 28.5 percent. It is also interesting to note that the number of adjudicated and delinquents did not vary: It was ± 5,500 in 1965 and ± 6,000 on 1975. While in 1965, 18 percent of them were placed in a juvenile prison or correctional institution, this percentage was practically the same, that is 17.2 percent in 1975.

The great reduction in the proportion of children placed in institutions refers to children under guardianship. The absolute number of this category of children declined from ± 19,000 in 1967 to ± 12,000 in 1976. But still more significant, the proportion of institutional placements has been dropping from 42 to 28 percent during that same period. Relatively more children go on living with their families or are placed in foster families or elsewhere.

So we may conclude this section stating, first, that considerably fewer children enter the Dutch child care and protection system now than they did some ten years ago, and second, that there is a sizable reduction in the placement of children whose parents are deprived or released of their parental rights. Moreover, it should be clear that the Dutch child protection system handles both outright delinquent children as well as problem children, who are habitual truants, repeatedly run away or are incorrigibile which are not considered as offenses by Dutch law.

THE PREVENTION OF DELINQUENCY

In this section I will concentrate on the prevention of delinquent behavior, and not on the prevention of "problem" behavior in general. It is necessary to limit the scope of the subject because "problem" behavior covers a large field of all kinds of disorders which can be prevented or treated by an extended network of health services, child guidance clinics, youth psychiatric clinics, and social service agencies. These institutions in many cases do offer help when asked to do so, but their services are extended to Dutch youth in general, and not to the specific subgroup that may enter the child care and protection system.

The selection of the institutions studied here is determined by my definition of delinquency prevention: the whole of efforts undertaken to avoid that a juvenile starts a delinquent career, or becomes engaged in a delinquent subculture. So the institutions I would like to examine are the school system, the police, the so-called "alternative" social agencies, and the day care centers. They all do preventive work, some of them within, others outside the system of juvenile justice. Studying their activities, we will dwell on the differences in approach, but we will also try to discover some important developments and new trends in delinquency prevention that all of them rely upon.

90

THE SCHOOLS AND DELINQUENCY PREVENTION

Many criminologists have stressed the importance of the school in the life of children and the effects of poor school performance on juvenile behavior. Indeed we have, starting with the Gluecks,[2] an increasing amount of empirical evidence indicating the relation of poor school records, repeating classes, and truancy with juvenile delinquency. Of course much of the research on juvenile delinquency has been done on recorded, often institutionalized, delinquents, which makes it very difficult to distinguish between causes and effects. But even research on representative group of juveniles has shown similar relations.[3] A study on hidden delinquency in a Belgian city, showed a strong relationship between truancy, punishment, time required for homework, and classes and a number of repeated and delinquent acts. It appears that high contributions are given by frequency of truancy, punishment by teachers and time spent on homework. The last item measured commitment to the school and its principal values. Persistant class repeaters get punished more often, play more often and dislike school much more, all of which variables are related to delinquency.

THE DUTCH EDUCATIONAL
STIMULATION PROGRAM

A rather recent initiative has been taken by the Ministry of Education and Sciences in cooperation with the Ministry of Culture, Recreation and Social Work. The program is called: "Educational stimulation program on behalf of children with developmental lags." The program provides additional means and support to schools in areas that suffer economic problems, slum areas in the larger cities and schools that have a large population of children of migrant workers and of children of color. The policy memorandum of the Ministry of Education and Sciences says: "the objective of the educational stimulation policy is to devise measures within, and in relation to the educational system, to eliminate or decrease lags in educational opportunities of deprived children, in order to give them—not only formally but in reality—the same opportunities as children in more favorable living conditions.''⁵ Not all socio-economic problems can be directly influenced by the Ministry of Education and Sciences, but they might be ameliorated by the following methods.

1. Reduce language lags, stimulate language development.

2. Influence cognitive, emotional, social and expressive functioning, to promote optimal conditions for growth.

3. To make it clear to teachers in what way discrepancy between family and school setting has adverse effects on childrens development, and teach them how to reduce this discrepancy.

4. Affect values and educational behavior of parents to the effect that they will pay more conscious attention to their children's development, and get more interested in their school education.

5. Influence environment conditions in general, by ameliorating the social-cultural situation and the housing and living situation as far as they are related to school education.

The first three objectives are predominantly the concern of the Ministry of Education and Sciences. The fourth objective is the responsibility of the Ministry of Culture, Recreation and Social Work and the fifth of both the Ministry of Culture, Recreation and Social Work and the Ministry of Housing and Physical Planning.

Which schools are selected for special supportive measures? In view of the difficulty of establishing objective criteria to determine educational priority schools and areas, the Dutch Ministry considers two criteria: 1. parents profession and 2. the number of the school's pupils going on to secondary education. Because the second criterion fluctuates and is subject to many inaccuracies, the parents' profession appears to be the most reliable point to consider. We have to add that these criteria are handled with some flexibility. Some low scoring schools need help because of other circumstances, such as being isolated or having a large number of children from our ex-colonies or of migrant workers as students.

In 1977 about 2,000 schools were in the program: about 1900 primary schools and 600 kindergarten schools, or 20 percent of all primary schools and 10 percent of all kindergartens. Moreover five regions have been selected for special stimulation projects. One is the city of Groningen in the northeast of the Netherlands where the educational and welfare systems are cooperating, as well as the community and the state university. Another is in the eastern mining area, which is an area in need of economic restructuring. There are already 100 schools in this region. Helmond in the southeast of the Netherlands is a slum city with great social and economic problems with 40 schools. The economically underdeveloped province of Drente in the northeast. The city of the Hague. Although there had been 69 schools in the program, it has recently started an integrated program, in which 110 schools participate. The two Ministries are implementing a generalized and integrated approach for all selected schools to orient educational *improvements* within the school. Extra teachers are provided on the express condition that improvements will be made such as improving guidance with school guidance services and innovations to provide individual help. Refresher courses for teachers are offered, as well as additional teaching material. *Welfare work within the school setting* also is being carried out, with home visits and parent meetings and by means of working with groups of parents to stimulate and modify educational behavior, eventually in collaboration with neighborhood organizations. Welfare work is being conducted outside the school setting but in coordination with the school for children below the age of 4 and for those over age 4 with their parents. Neighborhood social work is coordinated and school social work: the former is oriented to the relationship between the school and other organizations; the latter is addressed towards the individual.

SPECIAL YOUTH CARE

Special Youth care is provided by a system of 21 boarding schools to which children with school and family problems are referred by different social agencies (but not by juvenile court). The schools are subsidized by the Ministry of Culture, Recreation and Social work; they do not depend in any way on the Department of Justice. The general objective of Special Youth care is to give assistance to children who got stuck by a combination of social and pedagogical factors, in order to help them gain their own place in society.[9] Contrary to most other institutions the boarding schools offer "situations in an intentional and planned way, so the child will learn to help itself, to classify and objectify his world and to participate in social life in an independent, creative and critical manner." Put in such general way this objective is hardly any different from other programs that stress personal, social, creative, and human values. However, these schools deal with deviant children, children who feel they have failed, and are thus banned to special institutions.

Special Youth care therefore sees as its basic function to promote the self-realization of the child by surrounding it with a climate where it feels secure and accepted for what it is.

A particular dilemma is that our society's educational system is oriented to the continuity of the school career and the transmission of cultural values. One of the consequences of this orientation is that most institutional objectives are formulated in terms of "normalizing behavior" of "motivating for a school career", thus emphasizing conformity and adaptation to society's rules. Special Youth care is not in favor of such forced adaptation. It specifies that it wants programs, based on the life situation of the child determined by norms and values specific of his own subculture which is dominated by parents and peers.

Children are referred for special youth care by agencies for social work, school counseling and guidance services, doctors, the schools themselves, psychologic and psychiatric clinics.[6] As stated before, the schools do not deal with children from the juvenile protection system but with "children with study and behavior problems at school and at home," a category that could rather easily be covered by our Child care and protection system which states that a child can be placed under supervision if it is found "to be growing up in conditions in which it is exposed to moral or physical danger."

Covered by this program are children from eight to 18 years of age with a set of interrelated problems including bad housing, large families, overcrowding, low income, divorced parents, disturbed parents, or such organic factors as mild brain damage. Older children also may suffer from authority and identity conflicts including resistance to prolonged compulsory education and a desire to get away from parents without the ability to do so. They cannot meet the demands of achievement and competition in our society. These problems are mostly expressed in such behavior as quarreling, aggression, introversion, running away from home or from work, truancy, inability to play, unreliability, and so on.

On a yearly basis about a 1000 children are served by special youth care, which is a relative increase, since 1967, due essentially to changes in general views on the ways our child care and protection system should operate. In turn the number of children has decreased.

As placement in the boarding school is voluntary and therefore the collaboration of parents is very important as a condition for success. Though the schools admit retarded children, they will not deal with the serious mentally handicapped nor will they accept seriously disturbed and psychopathic children. Most of the children that are accepted have adjustment problems in school and family, as well as behavior problems that impair the adequate functioning of the child in the school, in its peer group and in the family. In addition, most of the children come from families with low incomes, of which a high proportion receive social welfare funds. Also, a high percentage of the children are from one-parent families, and a great number from large families.

As in most sectors of welfare work, institutional treatment, social work or social experimentation, evaluation is rather difficult. However, the boarding schools of special youth care try to evaluate their programs by means of interviews with the children or a questionnaire; sometimes the same is done with parents, and in some cases teachers or the referring agencies are asked for their opinion. In this way follow-up data were collected for 700 children during the period of 1969–1975. According to the—as they put it—"more or less objective data" the objectives have been reached in about 75 percent of cases.

THE CHILDREN'S POLICE IN THE NETHERLANDS

The Dutch child care and protection system dates from 1901, when the first Children's Acts were voted by Parliament. The new legislation provided the possibility to resort to civil instead of penal measures with respect to children. One of the consequences of the legislation was the creation of special police officers who would handle exclusively children's cases. The initiative was taken by the feminist movement which required that the new function would be held by a woman. (The same applies to the whole of the Child Protection Movement: see Anthony M. Platt, *The Child Savers,* University of Chicago Press, 1969.) Traditionally the children's police had a large social task. They visited foster families, picked up abandoned and maltreated children, controlled truancy, made social inquires for the court, looked after unwed mothers, looked for placement of children. These tasks underwent considerable change after World War II for essentially two reasons. The first reason has been the development of an expanding network of social services and welfare agencies, which took over a lot of services first supplied for by the police; the second reason is the delegation to the police of two new important tasks: the tracing of missing minors and the handling of penal cases implicating minors. The children's police have the tasks of the handling of penal cases against minors, the detection of missing and run-away youngsters, and the handling of social problems regarding minors (civil cases).

As far as the preventive activities of the police are concerned, we have to distinguish two levels of police intervention. Because they go out on the streets, the uniformed police often have the first contacts with minors. The children's police constitute part of the detective section: they have no patrol task but work at the police station. So we may say that generally the children's police handle cases that already have had some processing. With respect to the way the police handle their discretionary power, that is, decide what kind of action they will take, it is useful to make a distinction between penal offenders and what the Americans call "status-offenders." The first group is composed of youngsters that have committed an offense; the second group includes children who run away, who are "incorrigible," or habitual truants. These infractions are related to their status as a minor and would not be considered infractions if committed by adults.

As far as criminal offenses are concerned there are research results indicating that the police use several criteria when deciding to take a certain kind of action. American researchers found that the decision to make an official report and to take a youngster to the police station, was influenced by the seriousness of the offense and by the boy's outlook and behavior. In my own research in a Belgian city I found that the most important reason that children were taken into custody was related to the seriousness and frequency of delinquent behavior. However, other factors played a part in influencing the police (and prosecutors) decision, among which are socio-economic status, sex and ethnic origin. A Dutch study on the children's police concluded that children were arrested because of the seriousness of the offense, past contacts with the police, and the fact that they had left school. Moreover we know that in some police departments it is customary not to make a report of a minor offense if the offender has come into contact with the police for the first time. Only a simple note is made for police use. Should the youngster ever be caught again, then a formal report, together with the first note, is sent to the prosecutor. The policy reflects the efforts made by the police to keep youngsters out of the judicial circuit as long as possible.

Although there is of course considerable local variation, the police's attitude towards status offenders, including run-away kids, incorrigibles, truants, has changed from a rigid moralistic and repressive intervention to a far more tolerant, understanding, and preventive approach. Not only do they try to handle many of these cases in an unofficial and informal way, but they are also more inclined to refer and collaborate with other social agencies, even the so-called "alternative" ones that work with the same type of youngsters. It must be said that this has been a difficult and sometimes painful process, and conflicts could not be avoided. Moreover there are still legal and competency problems, but by and large the police tend to feel (as well as the prosecutor and the juvenile judge) that their legal and social agencies often cannot help children. So if there are other agencies which can, so much the better for all parties concerned!

I think we may conclude that the police play an extremely important role in preventing delinquency in a rather restricted way. Although they generally cannot do much in the area of combating causes of delinquency (however you define them) they try to solve certain problems or at least not to make bad things worse by handling cases informally. The rationale of this behavior is the feeling that making a youngster enter in the juvenile justice system, more often than not will make him only more delinquent.

ALTERNATIVE SOCIAL ASSISTANCE FOR YOUNG PEOPLE

The prevention of delinquency is not only a matter for official and professional institutions. Next to these institutions numerous so-called "alternative" social agencies came into existence at the end of the sixties: information centers for young people, as well as agencies that provided social and legal assistance and presented practical solutions to pressing problems. Born out of definite dissatisfaction with official social work agencies, these new centers attracted young people that could not find help anywhere else: children who had run away from home or from an institution, youngsters with alcohol or drug problems, girls wanting an abortion, young men who objected to military service, young people who did want to live on their own and did not know how to do so.

Now why is it that this type of agency did flourish in all the large cities? In what way do they differ from the traditional social work agencies? To me, it seems that they differ in two important respects: first in their conception of what constitutes a social problem and thus social work response; and second in the way they approach their clients. Characteristic of the traditional social work agency is its view of the client as having a problem, and of social work as helping their client to adapt and adjust to an outside situation. In other words, the situation being basically unchangeable, the client has to be changed. In this view the social order is accepted whereas the client is seen as an individual poorly adapted to the social order, may easily lead to "deviant behavior."[9] This conception of social work as well as the definition of what constitutes a problem has had some unfavorable consequences: the client is easily perceived as a troublemaker who should be made to adjust to the existing social order as quickly as possible and to obey its laws. As a result, the client tends to be treated as an object of efforts and care instead of as a partner in a helping relation. This, in turn, has led to an estrangement between the helper and client, and to bureaucratization of social work. The new philosophy of "alternative" social workers is entirely different. First of all, they view our social order as the principal cause of their clients many problems. It is not the client who is "deviant" or "sick," but the society in which he lives. So one of the objectives of this type of social work is to make their clients realize that much of their problems lie in the social order and should be resolved by adequate social action (for instance more employment, housing and educational possibilities for young people).

Contrary to the tendency in traditional social work towards professionalization, alternative agencies employ many volunteers noticed for their idealism and a critical attitude towards the social order. Many essential differences in the way they work distinguish them from the official organization. Initiative for help seeking is always originated by the client himself and not by any authorities (parents, school, police). Asking for help does not imply one has to give his name: anonymity is guaranteed and some agencies do not even keep a card system so as to prevent any official control of their activities. As a result, many youngsters who have a deep mistrust of official social agencies turn to them when they are in a mess. Related to this is the fact that the problem is examined as it is defined by the client and not by some abstract social standard. It is the client's problem as he sees it. This in turn implies that steps towards a solution of the problem are taken with the client's full consent and after consultation. The client is considered as an autonomous and responsible person. There is no room for paternalistic attitudes and the problem-solving process takes place in an atmosphere of complete equality. Another characteristic is a value-free and nonmoralizing attitude. The social workers do not want to maintain society's value-system but recognize the juveniles searching for new values. The point of departure is: "This is the society in which you are living with its rules and norms; these are the risks you take if you don't want to obey some of the rules and live your own life: so what shall we do?" It is an undeniable fact that this cool, realistic and nonmoralizing approach meets with an enthusiastic response among adolescents.

To conclude I would like to present an example of alternative intervention in the case of run-away children, a problem that occurs frequently. The example is based on the experience of a crisis intervention unit in Amsterdam, which dealt with children between 14 to 24 years. About 65 percent of them had some high school education, 45 percent had run away from their family, 30 percent from a home or child care institution. Clients were referred to the unit by juvenile information centers, the children's police, or the guardianship societies. A major characterisitc of the run-away juveniles was that they were living in a very autocratic educational setting. Norms and rules are established by the parents (or home) without any consideration of the child. To enforce these norms and rules, parents use every means in their power, even violence. They allow few initiatives or independence in their children, and even try to influence their behavior outside as well as within the home. Though the children seem openly compliant they are often rebellious and impulsive and are not able to make decisions and then bear the consequences of their actions. The same situation prevails in the generally large institutions from which the run-away juveniles come. This situation causes several problems for the crisis intervention unit. Their intervention is often seen by the parents as an infringement of parental authority, and thus the members of the unit are rejected. The parents frequently call the police and break up the relationship with son or daughter.

Because the capacity of the run-away youngster to make choices in an independent manner and take responsible decisions is seriously impaired, the unit has to take this into consideration. The objective of the agency is to help the juvenile (in a limited time of about 10 days) to find a provisional and experimental solution to the most pressing problems. In practice this may mean to restore the communication between juvenile and parents or home and to promote the juvenile's participation in decisions about his future. If the situation cannot be redressed this way, a new situation has to be created: this may imply a new place to live, or a new school or job. If necessary, contracts are established with long-term social assistance agencies , to ensure guidance for a longer period.

The following guidelines are viewed as essential for this kind of intervention. The unit must look for *a practical solution* to *pressing problems.* The solutions should be the basis for a new evolution, but being experimental by nature allowance should be made for failure. The environment should be agreeable and tolerant, but also activating and stimulating. The juvenile should be allowed to decide his future, but given his shortcomings in this respect, the unit should help him to find out what it is he really wants to do. The juvenile should be allowed to try out other forms of communication with adults and peers. Consider-

101

ing most juvenile's educational backgrounds, the unit should be able to give guidance to parents and educators. The unit should be able to supply long-term guidance for the juvenile (and his parents.)

DISCUSSION AND CONCLUSIONS

In this section I discuss four major institutions with respect to their role in delinquency prevention. Of all the institutions I reviewed, the governments efforts in the field of education no doubt represent the most direct and large-scale approach to the problem of delinquency. This ambitious program has the purpose to achieve a real impact on the school conditions that are so strongly correlated with delinquency: lack of ability to strive in the school system and to be successful. The program shows an awareness of the fact that children who function well and are happy in the most important social system (which figures as a future model of the adult social world) usually are not delinquent. The program could be defined as real prevention. It is clear that intervention by the police cannot have the same pretentions. They try to offer assistance in cases where things have already gone out of control. It is of course very difficult to evaluate how successful they are in their efforts to help children and to keep them out of court. However I would like to stress the fact that they do not see their function exclusively repressive, but fully accept a preventive role.

The "alternative" social agencies try to help their clients resolve problems in the most direct and practical way. As their views on the social order are mostly critical, the question of how and when to involve judicial authorities is rarely something worth considering. What distinguishes them most from the other institutions is the principle that nothing is done or decided without the clients consent and full participation.

Are we to conclude then that all these efforts in delinquency prevention have nothing in common and do not rest on some basic underpinnings? Fortunately this is not the case and we might even defend the viewpoint that they have influenced each other to reach a mutual understanding. Two basic principles shared by most agencies guide actual prevention activities and reflect a new way of considering the delinquency problem. The first principle (as it seems to me) presents a different way of looking at delinquent behavior. Not so long ago a boy defined as a delinquent was considerred either as a "bad" boy or as having deep-seated personality problems. Nowadays we tend to speak less about delinquents, but more about delinquent behavior. In some cases the behavior is symptomatic of family or school problems; in other cases it is just a reflection of a phase in the adolescent's life which is overcome when adulthood approaches. The point I want to make here is that in most cases delinquent behavior is conceived as related to some problems in the living environment of the juvenile; if one succeeds in solving those problems it is more than likely that the delinquent behavior will disappear. Now it is easy to see that in this conception prevention plays a major role. Assisting the juvenile to solve his problems, be it in the family or society becomes then an important task.

This brings us to the second principle that tells us that we should do almost anything to avoid involving the youngster in the juvenile justice system. Following criminological research in this respect it is felt that involvement in the juvenile system really makes one a delinquent by defining one that way. As a youngster cannot easily get rid of this "stigma," he finally ends up believing he is a real delinquent and so acts like one. Another harmful consequence of placing a child in an institution is that he will become involved in a delinquent sub-culture, where delinquent behavior is admired and encouraged. All this makes conforming to society later on extremely difficult.

So let us conclude this section by presenting a new definition of prevention on which most agenices would agree: "Delinquency prevention encompasses all activities destined to solve specific problems related to the social integration of the juvenile, and leaves out actions that would harm that integration by setting the juvenile apart from his peers."

INTERVENTION BY THE CHILD CARE AND PROTECTION SYSTEM

When problems grow out of hand and the child cannot cope with them, then official intervention may be the only possible way out. Several institutions deal with juveniles in different ways. Some of them use preventive measures as well as repressive measures; that is they may refer youngsters to extra-judicial agencies, or they may feel they must be sent to court. This is true for the children's police as well as the councils for child care and protection. Other institutions, which form the core of our protection system, will be treated in this section, that is, the juvenile judge, the guardianship societies and the family guardianship societies.

THE CHILDREN'S POLICE

In many instances the police are the first to deal with children who are in trouble. As I have mentioned before they refer the children to either the councils for child protection or the court.

THE COUNCILS FOR CHILD PROTECTION

In 1901 the Children's Acts created a new government institution called the Guardianship Council. This council formed a link between public authorities and the private organizations of child protection. Its advice to the juvenile court was required in all cases where the removal of the child or deprivation of parental rights was considered necessary. In 1956 19 Councils for Child protection were established, one in each court district and its responsibilities have been enlarged. The principle tasks of the actual councils are to: collect information in cases where measures are considered regarding parental authority (divorce, adoption, deprivation of rights) or prosecution of a minor. They supervise the execution of the orders of the juvenile judges by institutions or foster parents. They provide documentation and information on all matters relating to child care and protection in their district.

To understand the role of the actual councils we have to look at the way the councils have developed in the last 20 years. The original guardianship councils were created to form some sort of prosecution office in cases of minors. The board of administrators decided in each case what kind of action would be appropriate. However the founders of the new councils'decided that the task of recommending and presenting cases before the court should be done by professionals, that is, by trained social workers. This decision had two major consequences. One is that the social workers slowly developed a sense of role conflict due to the difficulty of serving two clients: the judicial authorities on one side and their young client (or family) on the other side. The second consequence is that more and more emphasis was put on social assistance on a voluntary basis, with full cooperation of the parties involved. Two other important developments contributed to change the council's tasks. Since 1956 numerous civil-law cases have been assigned to the councils: they handle now more civil than penal cases (divorce, adoption, guardianship). At the same time, influenced by recent criminological research, more and more people in the juvenile justice system became disillusioned with the way the system operated. As I have shown before, many people were convinced that judicial intervention is not in itself the solution to the delinquency problem, whereas on the individual level very often it does more harm than good.

If we consider judicial intervention as an endless selection process on different levels (the police, the councils, the prosecutor, the juvenile judge, the juvenile institutions, the Ministry of Justice), then we see a clear tendency of the practitioners at the various levels to keep as many children out of the juvenile justice system as possible. For the Councils of Child protection this means that their demands for a court measure have dropped from about 40,000 in the sixties to some 23,000 in 1976, whereas their social advisory task in civil matters has been gaining in importance.[13] Now, of course, this does not mean that the workload of the councils have been reduced, but what it does mean is quite a different conception of what the councils' task should be. The social workers within the councils do not consider their job as only some form of information gathering. They feel that they should supply guidance and counseling and help youngsters in trouble. The following elements characterize social work within the councils. The social worker tries together with the youngster, to find a solution to specific problems. Then the worker tries to make all parties concerned accept the proposed solution on behalf of the minor. If possible, social assistance is provided for on a voluntary basis, for instance by referring the child to another social agency. When a judicial measure seems unavoidable, indications are given for further social or thera-peutic intervention.

By emphasizing these elements in their work, the councils are able to reduce court intervention to a minimum and to demand a court action only in those cases where the parents absolutely re-fuse to collaborate in the solution of their child's problems.

I think it is clear that the councils during this century have been changed. From a prosecutional office they developed into an institution with a much wider social mission. As a result, only about 25 percent of all cases treated by the councils end up in the juvenile court.

THE JUVENILE JUDGE

The juvenile judge can take two different measures: a civil measure or a penal measure. A *civil measure* is taken when there is evidence that the parents of the child don't fulfill their paren-tal obligations. The judge may order one of three possible mea-sures, to remove the child from his parents when there is evi-dence of serious abuses, ill-treatment, deprivation; release from parental rights when parents appear to be unable or unfit to edu-cate their children; and to supervise the child if he is "threatened with moral or physical danger." The last category encompasses what is called status offenses in the United States, and includes truancy, running away, and the like. These are not considered as offenses in the Netherlands.

Child protection measures for noncriminal misbehavior are

authorized by criteria comparable to proceedings in the United States over questions of dependency and neglect. What is a similar situation in both countries is the extreme vagueness of the criteria applied. The authorities have considerable discretion in evaluating whether the facts indicate a "state of moral or physical danger" of the child, or whether he should be labeled a delinquent. However, there are different ways in which countries process children through their child protection system. Referring to a comparative study on five Western European countries it appears that in some of the countries jurisdiction in these matters is in Child Welfare Boards (local administrative agencies) (as in Sweden), whereas in the continental countries these cases are handled by a specialized children's judge (the Netherlands and France) or by a family court (West Germany).

An important point here is that the leading principle of action in all the countries is "the protection in the best interest of the child." This principle has in most countries led to a weakening of the procedural position of the child. Recently—and especially in the United States (in the Gault case)—there has been a critical reaction with respect to this situation, and slowly more safeguards for due process are being introduced (the hearing of the child, the presence of a council). There exists, however, substantial differences between European countries. In the Netherlands, the juvenile has hardly any rights during proceedings. In West Germany both the parents and the juvenile must be heard. In France they both have a right to be represented by council. In the United Kingdom juvenile proceedings are very much like adult proceedings. Also in the Netherlands the juvenile has no right to appeal at all, whereas in West Germany he cannot introduce an appeal if he is under the age of 14 years. Only in France does the juvenile himself have an unqualified right to appeal.

What are the measures applied in cases where children are "threatened by physical or moral danger"? In the Netherlands, France, and West Germany, the measures imposed are called "supervision" and "assistance in upbringing." But there are differences in the organization of the courts involved. Both in

West Germany and the Netherlands the court may appoint a "family guardian" who gives the parents directives concerning the raising and care of the child in question, and helps and counsels the child in whatever problems there may be. In France either an individual or an agency may be appointed to help and counsel the family. All the countries provide for the possibility of placing the juvenile outside his home in a foster family or institution whenever the desired objectives are not reached.

A *penal measure* is ordered when a minor is found guilty of a criminal offense. The law distinguishes between penalties and penal child protection measures. The penalty may include a reprimand, a fine, detention for a maximum period of 14 days, which the minor may undergo during weekends or on free afternoons (since 1965), and detention in a state correctional institution for a maximum period of six months. A penal measure of protection may consist of placement in an institution for special treatment (in the case of mental deficiencies), supervision or the child can be put at the disposal of the government (till its majority), which means placement in an approved school or in a foster family.

GUARDIANSHIP AND FAMILY
GUARDIANSHIP SOCIETIES

When the juvenile judge orders that parents be deprived of their rights to their child, the child is placed under the care of a guardianship society. This society is then completely responsible for the health, education, and instruction of the child and can decide to place the child in a home, an institution, or a foster family. All these decisions are taken without judicial intervention, and neither parents nor child have the right to appeal a decision of the guardianship society. In other words, the societies have large responsibilities as well as much discretionary power. In practice, however, children placed under supervision can be placed in institutions. The ultimate decision, in this case, is with the juvenile judge. There are some differences between family guardianship societies and guardianship societies. Family guardianship societies work with volunteers as family guardians. Guardianship societies decide on the extent to which parents will be allowed access to their children. Their social workers in general have less contact with parents, as in most cases children are placed in institutions.

DISCUSSION AND CONCLUSIONS

Both the child protection councils and the guardianship societies have come under heavy criticism since the sixties. The child protection council obviously operates mostly in conflict and stress situations. It may act as an advisor, a mediator, or instigate court action. However, it usually takes a long time before the interested parties know what will happen to them. Much confusion comes from the fact that most of the councils' collaborators are social workers. Many people therefore expect the council to function like a social service agency, and are very disappointed when it does not. Much irritation is caused by the fact that, in practice, the social reports made by the councils to inform the prosecutor or the juvenile judge cannot be consulted by the parents. Some of the councils have taken action to inform the parents as soon as the report is completed, but most councils are resistant to a more open attitude towards parents.

As far as the guardianship societies are concerned there is a growing opposition to their large discretionary power, and the lack of control on their decision. Some suggestions have been made to increase control on the decisions of the societies. A minor of 16 years or older should have the possibility, in case of conflict with a guardianship society (for example on placement in an institution) to address himself to the juvenile judge, who then should make the ultimate decision. The guardianship society should make a yearly report on its policy regarding each of the minors under its care, and address the report to the council of child protection. This would enable the council to involve the juvenile judge in cases of evidence of abuses.

Concluding this section, it is interesting to note that the trend in many European countries is to differentiate less rather than more among various categories of offenders. In Europe more emphasis is given (and perhaps more money and more provisions) to protecting and educating, and this value orientation entails more discretion and more measures imposed "for the best interest of the child."

TREATMENT AND REEDUCATION

Until the sixties, if a child was drawn into the child care and protection system, the chances were great he would end up in some sort of institution. As we have seen, this is no longer the case. From 1960 on, the proportion of children placed in institutions has been dropping, and many of the homes have been closed. This movement has been accompanied by a search for alternative measures like ambulatory treatment, semi-residential treatment, halfway houses and other experiments which I will treat briefly in this report.

Despite the new trends in child care, institutional treatment still remains a very important resource of the child protection system. Moreover, it is clear that we will always have a category of children that cannot go on living with their families and that must find a place in an institution. As institutional care will continue to be one of the major measures, it is all the more necessary to evaluate our institutional treatment programs in order to discover what works and what does not, and for what categories of children.

INSTITUTIONAL CARE IN THE NETHERLANDS

Our institutions are descendants of the orphanages where children were taught to adapt to society and to show gratitude to the community. Their objective was to help children but in a closed setting. They were situated in the inner city or at the outskirts of the city. Gradually, however, the parents as well as the city environment came to be considered bad for the children and they were taken from their family environment and placed in the "pure" countryside, where contacts with nature were expected to improve their dispositions.

Present institutions place great emphasis on "group education" by experts as well as the involvement of parents. In some institutions the social worker tries to develop some family treatment; at least he tries to maintain contact with the families of the children placed in the institution.

The objective of the homes is to promote and stimulate personality growth, socialization, and integration in society. Methods used vary from a strict pedagogical climate to a tolerant one, from systematic intervention to a more intuitive approach. The older youngsters often live in small homes, most of which were created after World War II. A minority of these homes are serving children with serious psychosocial problems. It is felt that these children with such serious problems need a more intensive and expert approach. Thus, although the overall objectives are the same as those of the other institutions, methods differ. More use is made of the services of psychologists and psychiatrists. There is, however, much variation in treatment methods: some of the homes use psycho-dynamic treatment, others use behavior modification, Rogerian principles, the interactionist of orthopedagogical approach.

There are a number of special boarding schools for children with family *and* school problems. There also are social-medical homes for children with physical disabilities; homes for the mentally handicapped or for children with mild brain damage; observation homes to achieve better diagnosis and more effective placement; crisis centers that receive youngsters with specific problems such as drugs for a limited time.

SOME EVALUATIONS OF INSTITUTIONAL TREATMENT

Although the Netherlands have a large network of widely differentiated institutions, there have been hardly any attempts to evaluate their treatment in a scientific manner. Up until now, we have had only one scientific evaluation study on a psychiatric youth center[18] and a report of a special investigation commission on an institution for girls.[19]

Let us review briefly the results of the study and the commission's report in order to indicate some of the problems that confront institutional care. *The psychiatric youth center at Zandwijk* was created in 1957 for adolescent boys with emotional disorders and pathological behavior. All of them had committed offenses and were placed in the institution by the juvenile judge. Many of them had been living in other homes or foster families: 70 of the 90 boys had experienced different living arrangements before arriving at Zandwijk. The majority had shown a number of behavior problems within the family setting. More specific deviant behavior included vagrancy, habitual truancy, vandalism, thefts, aggressive delinquency, and sexual behavior problems. Many of them were school drop-outs, and had worked in unskilled jobs. Treatment objectives were vague: " . . . to promote the boy's possibilities to depend on himself, and to realize his intentional potentials with respect to his old environment and to his new freely chosen environment."

The methods used are relatively traditional and involve orthopedagogic influencing of the boy's daily life, which may imply all kinds of work activities, individual therapy once a week, group therapy, and family therapy by social work methods.

The objectives of the study can be summarized in the following questions. Which of the boys continued to show delinquent behavior or other behavior disorders and which ones abandoned this behavior after release from Zandwijk? What elements in the post-therapeutic environment promoted a favorable or unfavorable development? What elements in the treatment situation, in personality structure, or in the original environment promoted a favorable or unfavorable development.

The experimental group included 90 boys who had left Zandwijk 2 years before. The control group included 44 boys suited for Zandwijk treatment but not admitted because of lack of space. They had been staying in other institutions. As far as delinquency is concerned, all possible measures of delinquency as well as number of delinquent boys in both experimental and control group showed no difference in extent or seriousness of delinquent behavior: 80% of the ex Z-boys and 85% of the controls had recidivated within 2 years after leaving the institution. Significant differences in favor or the ex Z-group have been found with respect to development in work and leisure environment and as far as social relations with the enivronment are concerned. Ex Z-boys also seemed to appreciate their stay in the institution more, than did the control boys. No difference in the relationship with the life partner, or in scores on neuroticism. As for the effect of the orthopedagogic and psychotherapeutic treatment effects at the moment of release, effects are weak or non-existent. Although there are some differences in terms of a more favorable work and leisure orientation, these differences failed to show any relationship with delinquency.

The Heldring Foundations were founded in 1847 by the Rev. O.G. Heldring as a refuge for girls and young women that "were led astray." In the 1950s the old institution was changed to include a reception, an observation, an orthopedagogic home, and a youth psychiatric clinic. In the spring of 1974, a kind of organized pressure group for minors published a document criticizing different aspects of the institution (among them the authoritarian educational climate, the frequent use of isolation, medication, and cold showers). The pressure group organized a protest action and invasion of the institution; then two educators working in the institution were fired, and press and T.V. devoted much attention to the case. As a result, the foundation asked the State Secretary of Justice to appoint a commission to conduct an objective investigation into the institution's treatment conditions. The following is based on the findings of this commission[19]

The institution has a vague, not very consistent treatment philosophy based on the following principles. Bring *"structure" in the girls' lives.* This means that institutional life is dominated by rules and regulations. The day is organized by strict regulations on rising, eating, working, recreation, and sleeping times. The basic idea is that order and regularity offer these "chaotic" girls a simple, clear, nonstimulating living situation. When they would be able to master such situations, they would feel more secure and thus their self-confidence would be enhanced. Infraction of the rules is punished by different measures ranging from being sent to bed early to isolation. *Treatment is provided through the group.* The group represents society ordered by rules. By adapting to its norms and rules, girls are expected to develop the ability to adapt to society's norms and rules. *Close relations between treatment personnel and girls are not encouraged.* Too close attachment is considered to be harmful to the children, especially in view of the fact that they eventually would be leaving the institution. Rules should be respected because they are rules, not out of sympathy for a group leader.

According to the findings of the commission, there has never been a well planned transition from a "custodial and converting home" to a treatment institution. The institution "just developed" without conscious choice. This resulted in a kind of inductive planning from within; scientific knowledge of treatment or experiments with new methods were never integrated. This means in practice that old routine was continued and old practices standardized. The question "what do we want, where do we go?" was rarely asked. This situation had several consequences. The institution continued to work out of ethical values instead of clearly formulated treatment objectives. The institution made no response to a number of changes in recent years such as the change in the population in care; a lack of sufficient means (no coherent plans could be presented to the subsidizing authorities); personnel changed from mostly female to mostly male professionals. The children were isolated from a so-called permissive society. As a result there was no connection between the institution and the larger society. The home was forced to deal with too many functions: reception, observation, treatment in open and closed sections, psychiatric treatment. The population consists of very difficult girls. But definitions of their problems are vague and unclear, for one reason, because there is no systematic knowledge concerning behavior and individual problems. There are no systematic treatment skills with respect to these different problems. Rather, the perceptions of the girls' problems are stereotyped. As a result, the group leaders suffer from feelings of powerlessness and lack of know-how and skills.

Thus the principle objective is "repressive regulation," that is, stating rules and punishment for breaking them. All this leaves little room for treatment. Concerning the different forms of therapies, there seems to be a lack of integration and coordination of group work, individual therapy, and the approach of the school.

With respect to both the principles of "relational distance" and "person related" therapy, the commission does not consider them favorable for treatment. Lack of communication and staff support as well as a lack of clear treatment objectives seem casually related to the application of these principles. However, the commission emphasized that most of the problems met by the Heldring foundations are shared by the other "terminal station" institutions as well as by those state institutions that have the same function. They all lack specific treatment objectives, clear criteria for accepting children, and a consistent treatment policy. They all get the most difficult children that are rejected by other institutions. They all lost touch with "real" life in outside society, and with new developments in social and scientific conceptions. It must be said that society as well as the human and social sciences have not offered enough help in achieving adequate treatment orientation.

CHANGES IN INSTITUTIONAL TREATMENT

It is of course no coincidence that there has been a dramatic reduction in placements in institutions by the juvenile court. So great is the disillusionment with the results of that policy that institutions themselves have been looking for new directions. The first important change is one of size: there is a clear tendency to rely upon smaller units. Some examples are: *family homes* of at most four children without extreme behavior disorders; at the moment there are about 30 of this type of home, directed by nonprofessionals, and *group homes* housing at most six juveniles directed by a small team of professionals. There are *Browndale houses* for seriously disturbed children. They house four to six children. We have about ten of these homes. *Intensive care units* are integrated in a large scale organization including foster homes. A professional staff treats serious behavior disorders. There are as yet only three of this type of home. There is in this country a definite lack of halfway houses, that is small homes which provide a transition between the institution and independant living arrangements. However, a growing number of small living units, such as hostels, or supervised lodgings for juveniles of 16 years and older, have been founded.

One of the dismaying consequences of living in the institutions is the total dependence of youngsters. They do not know how to budget either their income or their time; they cannot shop, nor cook, nor do their own washing or cleaning. In short, they are unable to live on their own, and this is specially harmful for those that cannot or do not want to return home.

It was felt that some kind of intermediate situation that would teach the adolescent to be independent and that would wean him from group living was necessary. For this purpose, *boarding houses* have been set up to give shelter to boys and girls of 16 years and older. The objective is to promote independence outside the group setting, which does not suit some personalities. It is a kind of a halfway stop between the institution and society. *Therapeutic units* (four to six adolescents) provide for intensive, individualized therapy. The units are housed in ordinary one-family houses, but are mostly part of a larger "mother organization." *Ortho-pedagogic units* provide for intensive relations with a supervisor, but no therapeutic treatment. The number of these units is growing rapidly (at this time there are 15 to 20 of this type of unit). *Training centers for independent living* group about 8 adolescents in a house or apartment, and provide a learning situation. *Supervised independent living*; in these cases there is no supervisor living with the youngsters. Guidance can be provided for but has to be asked for. Supervisors are often volunteers. This type of house—actually about 30—is also growing very rapidly.

Some of the residential institutions offer children a transition to society by allowing the juvenile to live outside the institution. The small unit provides for more time, quiet, and opportunity to react to potential problems. Also, problems are recognized more quickly, so help by staff is more immediate. There is a training for normal, good contacts with neighbors and visitors. As a result, juveniles have a greater motivation to attend school and find jobs. There is a greater sense of responsibility for the house, furniture, shopping, cooking, and cleaning, among other things. There is a training for normal, good contacts with neighbors and visitors. Adolescents are much better and more rapidly prepared to return home or go on living on their own, than was the case when they had to leave directly from the institution.[20]

The observation of 20 boys aged 16 to 18 years old, who were placed in residential institutions, showed the following results. Length of stay was about 7½ months. When the experiment was reported, 14 boys had left. Six boys went on living on their own; three boys returned to their parents; two boys went on to other lodgings; one boy returned to a conflictual home situation and one boy was reconvicted. That is, there were six real successes, six relative successes and two failures.[21] Of course, this constitutes in no way an evaluation of this type of institution. All we can say at the moment is that these new forms of intervention might offer new hope in the field of child care and protection in our country.

TREATMENT IN THE JUVENILE'S OWN ENVIRONMENT

In the last ten years the possibilities for young delinquents to get some form of therapy while staying at home have slowly been increased. The advantage of this kind of intervention is that one is working in the environment that created the problems in the first place (family, school, or work). One example of behavior therapy in such a setting has been undertaken by the Paedological Institute in Amsterdam.[22] The objective of the therapy was to teach a certain number of social skills that would enable the boys to cope better with some frequently occurring daily problems. Participation in the program was voluntary. The experimental group consisted of 29 boys, aged 14 to 20 years whose problem behavior expressed itself frequently in delinquency (ten boys had been staying in a state institution; 19 boys

117

had been put under a "supervision" order).

The first sessions are devoted to a careful analysis of behavior. Then all situations that create problems are attacked by discussion and role playing. Behavior is to be improved by so-called behavior rehearsal; use is made of video feedback. Then the juvenile must apply the trained behavior in reality and report back to the therapist. The therapy tries not to focus exclusively on verbal skills, but on concrete behavioral skills: how to solve conflicts without fighting; how to behave with parents, peers, persons of the opposite sex, colleagues, authorities. How to behave in school, work, cafe; how to behave in shops; how to dance; how to present oneself for a job; how to spend one's leisure time. The aim is to have one to four therapeutic sessions a week, but total treatment did not exceed three to four months. After a follow-up period of about 10 months, only seven of the 29 experimental boys had recidivated, against 20 of the 29 control boys, a very favorable result.

Another example is the growing number of daycare centers of which there are actually some 27.[23] A day care center admits 18 to 24 children, and employs, among others, two educationalists, a social worker, and often an ortho-pedagogue or a psychologist. Children are admitted with problem behavior of such a nature that parents cannot cope with it. Several instances like the child guidance services and the child care and protection system welcome these centers; they form very useful facilities for those children that would not get any profit from institutional treatment.

The daycare centers address themselves to the child and its family; then try to teach the children specific social skills, self-reliance and self-confidence. Results have been encouraging, even in the case of rather serious problem behavior (vandalism, incorrigeability, aggressive behavior, theft); school work also has been improved considerably. Parents are approached as "interested parties" and not as patients or clients. Discussions with them are not only analytical but also supportive, which promotes an effective collaboration between parents and the center. It is expected that this type of facility will grow in number in the near future, their most important quality being that the treatment does not imply family disintegration.

CONCLUSIONS

In this report on the Dutch child care and protection system we have tried to show some of its strengths and weaknesses. Let us now conclude by reviewing the major points of criticism. One serious criticism of the system is the lack of awareness of a minor's right as an individual. In fact, the law has put much emphasis on the rights of parents, but very little on the rights of minors. This orientation is apparent throughout our whole system. It shows in the power of the child protection council to request that a case should go to court, which is the same role as the prosecutors in penal law.

It also shows in the power of the juvenile judge to decide whether a child is in "physical or moral danger" or is a delinquent, as well as in the weak procedural position of the juvenile. Likewise, we have mentioned the nearly absolute power of the guardianship societies to decide on the child's life and the impossibility to appeal against its decisions.

The conclusion seems warranted that our whole system is based on the idea that children have to be protected, that parents, in the first place, and authorities, next, have only "the best interest of the child" in mind. Consequently there is no need to change the child's position in court, build in more guaranties for due process or enlarge its individual rights. But, it must be said, all this is now changing. Under the influence of liberalization and democratization movements in the sixties, the alternative social service agencies came into being. They had, in turn, a great impact on the official child protection system. As we have seen the police as well as the child protection councils considerable changed their approach and their philosophy; they developed far greater tolerance for deviant behavior, more respect for the individual, and more concern for solutions based on voluntary collaboration of the parties involved. However, this does not seem enough. Several reformers want to improve and guarantee legally the autonomy of minors from 12 years on. They propose that from the age of 12 years onwards, a juvenile should gradually be allowed to choose his own relations, to be a member of associations of his own choice, to choose his own medical doctor or social service, to determine his professional or other education, to choose his residence and to have his own partial income. In case of conflict with his parents he should have the right to address himself to the child protection council for mediation, if he is 12 to 16 years old, and to the juvenile judge if he is 16 years or older. These propositions that have not been adopted as yet, do clearly show a change in outlook on youthful behavior in general and on the problems that may rise between youth and society. It is essentially this change in outlook that will produce in the future profound modification of our child care and protection system.

A second serious criticism was articulated by the special investigation commission on the Heldring foundation, as they stated that most of our institutions have no clear objectives or policy about treatment and no clear idea of who exactly to treat. It seems obvious that there is a pressing need for research in this field either on the level of the individual institution or on state level. Therefore the commission made two recommendations. The national federation of private child care institutions (which include not only homes, but also family guardianship societies and foster home societies) should develop a large vision on treatment policy, its objectives and possible means, in collaboration with the authorities (Department of Justice, Health and Education). As private institutions are often more concerned about their own autonomy than about policy options, or treatment conceptions, there is an important role to be played by the official authorities and the federation in this respect. Also, a training center for workers in the field of child care and protection should be founded. The training center should promote collaboration between the universities and field workers. Thus new scientific theoretical developments and research findings would reach the field, and the field workers would provide continuous feedback and test out new ideas and approaches.

A third serious criticism is the fact that the actual child care and protection system, by its judicial character, has important and harmful stigmatizing effects on those who enter it. A special commission uniting members from different ministries has brought out a report in 1976 on an integrated policy on Youth Welfare. The commission recommended that a large integrated policy be formulated with respect to prevention, intervention, and social aid. This policy should be the concern of the Ministries of Economic Affairs, Housing, Health, Welfare and Culture, Education and Justice. Social services and child welfare should be regionalized and coordinated at the local level. Coordination between school doctors, guidance clinics, and teachers should ensure an early recognition of problem behavior so that more emphasis can be put on prevention of more serious troubles. It is not sure that the commission's recommendation will lead to rapid or drastic measures of change. Let us be honest: This kind of change comes only slowly. But it indicates the realization that—perfect as our system may seem to some—it has serious flaws.

Our society is not static but dynamic and changing. If we want our child protection system to function adequately, it is an absolute requirement that we adapt to the changes and allow for reforms and innovations. Fortunately there are hopeful signs that we will indeed succeed in doing so.

BIBLIOGRAPHY

1. Department of Child Care and Protection Ministry of Justice *Report* of the years 1975 and 1976.
2. S. and E. Glueck, Unraveling Juvenile Delinquency, (Cambridge, Mass: Harvard University Press, 1972).
3. Tr. Hirschi, *Causes of Delinquency,* Univ. of California Press, 1972
4. J. Junger-Tas, "Hidden Delinquency and Judicial Selection in Belgium," in *Youth Crime and Juvenile Justice,* P.C. Fri-

day and V.L. Stewart, eds. (New York: Praeger, 1977).

5. Ministry of Education and Sciences, *Beleidsplan voor het Onderwijs aan groepen in achterstandsituaties,* (Den Haag: Staatsuitgeverij, 1974).

6. Bijzondere Jeugdwerk Lochem, *Een schets van het Bijzonder Jeugdwerk in internaatsverband,* (Lochem, 1976).

7. M. Andriessen, *Kijken bij de kinderpolitie,* (Ijmuiden: Vermande en Zoon, 1976).

8. I. Piliavin and S. Briar, "Police Encounters with Juveniles," *American Journal of Sociology,* 70 (September 1974).

9. H. van Beugen: *Nieuwe ontweikkelingen in de hulpverlening,* Proces, no 2 (Februari 1977).

10. J. Junger-Tas; "Nieuwe ontwikkelingen in de Belgische jeugdberscherming," *Tijdschr. voor maatschappij vraagstukken en welzijnswerk, 28, 19* (November 1974).

11. A.C. Driessen and M.A.A. van der Veer; "Hulpverlening aan weggelopen jongeren in een krisiscentrum," *Maanblad Geestelijke Volksgenzondheid,* 28, 12 (1973).

12. C.W.E. Abbenhuis, *De Raad voor de Kinderscherming,* (Nationale Federatie voor de Kinderbescherming, 1968).

13. J.E. Doek; "Wat is een goede raad voor de toekomst?" *Openbare les* (Vrije Universiteit Amsterdam, September 1977).

14. C. Bolger-Schoenmakers: "Raden voor de Kinderbescherming, wat nu?" *Proces,* 2, 1 (1977).

15. F. le Poole; "Law and Practice Concerning the Counterparts of "Persons in Need of Supervision" in Some European Countries with a Particular Emphasis on the Netherlands," *in Lee E. Teitelbaum ed. Beyond Control, Status offenders in the Juvenile Court,"* (Cambridge, Mass. Ballinger Publishing Co. 1977).

16. J.E. Doek and S. Slagter, *Kinderbescherming in Nederland,* WIJN and Stichting voor het Kind, eds. (Amsterdam 1977).

17. P.A. de Ruyter and J.D. v.d. Ploeg, *Inrichtingswerk op een*

Nieuw Spoor, WIJN and de Stichting voor het Kind, eds. (1978).

18. M. Eijer, *Winst en verlies-resultaten van residentiele behandeling bij emotioneel gestoorde delinquente adolescenten (Naarden: Los, 1975).*

19. *Rapport van de commissie belast met een onderzoek naar het pedagogisch en psychiatrisch beleid der Heldringstichtingen* (1976).

20. K. Heslinga; "Zelfontplooiing van oudere meisjes met hulp van de Helper Haven, Maandbl. v.d. Geest," *Volksgezondheid,* 9 (1977).

21. A.J. Wijnands, "Helpen met de deur open bij de Lindenhof," *SJOW* (March 1974), pp. 99-107.

22. A.A.J. Bartels and J. Heiner: *Effecten van ambulante-gedragstherapie aan "delinquente" adolescenten,* (Amsterdam: Paedologisch Instituut, November 1977).

23. H. van Reenen, "Dagcentra voor schoolgaande jeugd in ontwikkeling," in *Facetten van Jeugdbescherming,* WIJN and Stichting voor het Kind, eds. (1976).

7

The Soviet Union

Stanislav V. Bordoin

Professor Borodin describes the holistic Soviet approach to child development in this thought-provoking, albeit somewhat controversial chapter. Coordination of home, school, and community is regarded as a natural consequence of responding positively to socialist philosophy. Delinquency is looked upon as an indicator of failure to apply basic precepts in the education of the child. The home and school, working together, are considered to be the two fundamental influences that determine the direction in which the child will develop. Recognition is given to the need for personalized attention to unresponding children, and professional assistance is made available when the need demands it. The community as a whole, reflecting socialist philosophy, influences the child toward obedience to the law. This is accomplished in many ways including the provision of "law consciousness" courses offered in the schools and universities, and through "parents' Saturdays" in the cinema when children along with their parents see special programs on the law, citizenship, and personal responsibility. Professor Borodin has given us an important accout of the Soviet system for dealing with juveniles who run afoul of the law. Readers who have wondered how delinquents have been dealt with in the USSR since the juvenile court

125

was abolished by Soviet legislation in 1935 will find the answers in this chapter. The reader will be interested to know about the existence of "public order strong points" and of widespread involvement of citizens in preventive programs.

Editor

The answer to the question about the causes of criminality is given by historical materialism, a science about general laws on human social development, created by K. Marx and F. Engels and developed by V.I. Lenin. Explaining the causes of criminality marxism-leninism proceed from the thesis that they are caused by antagonistic social-economic formations. V.I. Lenin wrote: "And, secondly, we know that the fundamental social cause of excesses which consist of violating the rules of social intercourse, is the exploitation of the masses, their want and their poverty. With the removal of this chief cause, excesses wil inevitably begin to "wither away". We do not know how quickly and in what order, but we know that they will wither away".

Hence, the main prerequisite for the "dying off" of the criminality is the elimination of exploitation, misery, and indigence of laborers. In the socialist society, as it has been noted, there is no exploitation of man by man; indigence, unemployment, misery, national oppression and race inequality are eliminated.

Explaining causes of criminality remaining at the stage of socialism, the Soviet criminology proceeds from K. Marx: "What we have to deal with here is a communist society, not as it has developed on its own foundations, but, on the contrary, just as it emerges from capitalist society, which is thus in every respect economically, morally and intellectually, still stamped with the birth marks of the old society from whose womb it emerges."

Hence, in consciousness of men, in life, in economical relations there remain remnants of capitalism, which even though they have no basis in socialist society, continue to influence certain members of society. The fact is that not all of the people at once realize the necessity to act according to the new conditions engendered by the new form of property and new productive relations. This is explained by the fact that social consciousness, as the reflection of social being, is relatively independent. The remnants of the past are revealed in various forms of social consciousness in the form of implanted habits, that is, prejudices, and habits of the past among other forces. For example, parasitism and "sponging" is an aspiration for using all the material and spiritual wealth without doing any work. They oppose radically the following principles of socialism: "If one doesn't work, he doesn't eat." "From each, according to his abilities; to each, according to his labor." In certain conditions, and very often because of the absence of control for the measure of labor and the measure of consumption, because of the tolerance to the manifestations of parasitism and sponging in industrial, social and family spheres, these phenomena lead to the mercenary and other crimes.

The preservation of the remnants of the past in people's minds and behavior is explained by the number of circumstances. From the philosophical point of view the persistence of the behavior of the past is explained by the fact that part of the social consciousness is lagging behind the social reality. This very fact explains why the social consciousness of some of the members of the society continues to reflect habits, traditions, and views which were typical for the former social system.

The influence of the bourgeois ideology favors the preservation of past behavior too, but the Soviet Union and other socialist countries strive against such influence, which is revealed in penetration from abroad of the ideas of exploitation, mercantilism, consumption, and various primitive instincts (for example pornography). Shortcomings in the work of state bodies and public organizations, some objective difficulties, and certain unresolved problems of building of our society favor the persistence of past bahavior as well.

So, the Soviet theory of criminology proceeds from the fact that general cases of all the crimes, which are remnants of the former social system, gradually will disappear as we build communism. The established, stable decrease in criminality in the Soviet Union, not only in the prewar period, but also during the postwar years, bears out the realization of this ideal in practice. We can see it from the following data on convictions: In 1975, for example, they decreased by 44.1 percent, as compared with the pre-war year of 1940. Convictions in 1975 decreased by 18 percent over 1958.

Not only quantitative but also qualitative changes have been made in the criminality structure. Professional criminality has been eliminated, cases of banditism has become a rarity. the Soviet society knows nothing of criminal actions resulting from misery, unemployment, deprival of one's share, class, and national inequality and oppression, since these phenomena are rooted out under socialism. There is no child homelessness to serve as a source of juvenile delinquency.

All these changes are objective, inherent features of socialist social order. They are conditioned by the whole process of development of the Soviet state, by a high level of maturity of the social relations of developed socialism, by the increase in the well-being, cultural level, and awareness of the population.

Only a small percentage of juveniles become criminals. The published data on some regions and republics show that this percentage vary from 3 or 4 to 9 or 10 percent, although in the cities it is higher.

The results achieved in the struggle against criminality, including juvenile delinquency, are the consequence of the implementation of directives of the Communist party of the Soviet Union to consolidate efforts of state and social organs to prevent offences. This is done by measures of persuasion and compulsion through educational and preventive measures.

At the same time, the above-mentioned fundamental thesis does not give an answer to the question why a crime is committed by one person and not by another. One can answer it only after investigating what conditions bring about crime and what

128

encourages criminality in individuals or what encourages criminal intent and the committing of crimes.

The majority of soviet scientists now agree on the causes of juvenile delinquency. There are specific causes for juvenile delinquency. First, we would like to stress that lately in the West industrialization and urbanization are frequently cited among the causes of juvenile delinquency. It is difficult to agree with such a position, though one may argue that it is to some degree confirmed by statistic data. The essence of our position here is as follows: Urbanization and industrialization could not be regarded as causes of juvenile delinquency, although they could engender negative social changes influencing their delinquency. That is, in the socialist society such an influence of urbanization and industrialization on criminality is not a direct one. It results from miscalculations of an administrative and managerial character concerning the struggle against criminality and other antisocial phenomena; these miscalculations may be prevented and eliminated.

This opinion has been confirmed in reality. In Kursk, Lvov, and Novgorod and in a number of other cities a decrease in juvenile delinquency has been achieved in spite of the growth of population; it is a result of active organizational work of Soviets of People's Deputies, the law enforcement agencies, the educational institutions, and the public organizations.

The causes of crime do not exist separately from an individual—the bearer of remnants of the past. This behavior, as far as juveniles are concerned, is brought about first of all by shortcomings in upbringing. The studies in juvenile delinquency also show that crimes are committed by those adolescents who have not received an adequate education. They do not follow a moral rule, elaborated in the process of education, not to comit antisocial actions. Their personality is characterized by a low moral level.

The remnants of past behavior in every day life are seen most clearly within the family frame, between parents on one side and children on the other side. The shortcomings of education of children in the family may be of different character, but among them there should be noted the most specific, which can be seen more frequently during the investigation of the nature of juvenile offences. According to the selective data the most common is the lack of enough attention and control from the parents' side towards the children's behavior.

The immoral behavior of parents: hard drinking, quarrels, fights, or the commitment of antisocial actions also adversely affects adolescents' education. A number of other shortcomings in the family may influence the behavior of the adolescents. That is, not all the parents prepare children for labor. Some of them say in such a way: "We have worked, let our children have a rest." These are the families where adolescent offenders come from.

The lack of parental authority and respect may lead to the situation when an adolescent becomes "sceptic" and falls under the influence of undesirable persons. It is difficult for parents to gain the regard of an adolescent, but to regain it is more difficult. Sometimes parents try to regain authority on a primitive artificial base, so-called "false authority." An interesting description of false authority has been given by the famous Soviet scientist-pedagogist A.S. Makarenka. For our investigation the most interesting to consider are "authority of suppression," "authority of affection," "authority of kindness," "authority of bribery," which are common in families of juvenile offenders.

The unfairness of parents influences juveniles in an extremely negative way, it antagonizes them against their family and makes them self-centered and unsociable. As a result of such unfair or cruel treatment, an adolescent sometimes will leave home and find himself on the way to commiting crimes.

It is known that side by side with the family an enormous educational function is accomplished by the school. The school sometimes corrects the shortcomings of the education in the family. But, at the same time, the school education has its own shortcomings. The individual approach to the adolescents in school is not always provided, though it is a necessary condition of a sound education. Frequently teachers, because of their lack of skills or a responsible attitude to their duties, do not always understand the specific characteristics of adolescents. The failure to teach the pupil so he can be promoted with his own age group is mainly explained by the lack of the individual approach. The results of the observation of schoolchildren—offenders show that they, in general, are older than their schoolmates. The questioning of juvenile offenders in Iksha reformatory demonstrated that 63 percent of them had fallen two to four years behind and 23 percent were five years behind.

There is almost no sex education offered by the schools. However it is one of the most "acute" problems. As a result, the adolescents receive the notions on sex from older friends and, as a rule, in a distorted form. In addition, the studies of juvenile offenders show that teachers in an overwhelming majority of cases did not show any interest in juveniles' behavior outside the school.

In order to answer the question why a certain crime is committed by one adolescent and not by another we must study the motivation of their actions. Usually, they have a tendency to imitate the actions of others and cannot judge good or bad actions.

When a crime is committed by a juvenile along with motives of self-interest, jealousy, revenge ruffianly purposes, characteristic for adults, there may be seen also the specific motives evidencing about tendency to follow a way of life non corresponding to one's possibilities, as well as motives of false romance, feelings of comradeship, erroneously understood, etc.

At the same time while studying juvenile delinquency causes it is necessary to consider that adolescents frequently do not realize fully the motives of their deeds. The point is that adolescents pay considerably more attention to the exterior side of offence than to the purpose and motives of its commitment. That is why the actions of juveniles do not always disclose the real reasons for the crime committed by them.

131

Incitement by adults is one of the causes of juvenile crime. Investigation shows that juveniles frequently commit offences after some older person has involved them in criminal activity (persuasion, intimidation, promise of protection, "lending" them money, or offering them liquor among other things). These persons are mostly ex-convicts, recidivists not willing to work after they are released from prison. To involve juveniles in criminal activity they also rely upon former acquaintances from the same houses, courtyards, schools, and streets. The overwhelming majority of instigators and organizers of juvenile criminal groups are persons two to three years older than the children they are influencing.

A negative influence is exerted on juveniles by those works of literature and films, especially of Western production, where one can see a veiled positive attitude towards the criminals. Some convey the idea that crime involves "courage," "honesty," "resourcefulness," and "nobleness" (perhaps irrespective of authors' will). The behavior of the criminal heroes of such works become an ideal for imitation by adolescents. In addition, the criminals seldom are opposed by really resourceful, brave, honest, and noble workers who devote their lives to the struggle against criminality. Even, at the least, some works that propagandize a "beautiful" carefree life consisting only of pleasures. Such films exert inauspicious influences on juveniles. They contribute to formation of anomalous conceptions of life contradicting the humanistic moral.

When analyzing the concrete reasons for juvenile delinquency it should be taken into consideration that crimes are committed as a result not of a single reason but a number of them. Also, when the base motives are established for crime commitment (revenge, self-interest, jealousy, or the influence of adults, or of works of art devoid of pinciples and ideals) there is always present a failure in education.

Soviet criminology unanimously agrees that there are concrete reasons for juvenile delinquency (as well as any delinquency).

Among the circumstances favoring juvenile delinquency there should be cited the following.

First, is is known that juveniles who do not or will not participate in organized forms of out-of-school activities under the supervision of parents or others might find themselves an occupation which is not always an inoffensive one. The studies show that every fifth juvenile offender is a schoolboy who committed a crime during hours he was free from classes. The other aspect if this problem consists is the fact, that juveniles who have dropped their studies do not always go to work or study in evening school. "Idleness" is favorable for delinquency.

Shortcomings in educational work among juveniles in the schools frequently encourage crime. The administration may pay insufficient attention to them. The juveniles may fall under the influence of the same workers who are drunkards, and shirkers, and who start "industrial" education with the appeal to squander "together on drink the first earnings, and teach the young worker how to deceive a foreman, or a chief of shop or a quality control inspector, among other things.

Drinking is one of the circumstances favoring the commitment of crimes by juveniles. Even the parents drinking can exert a negative influence on juveniles. Of course, juveniles may commit a crime in the state of intoxication. The examination of offenders in educational-labor colony in Bashkir ASSR showed that more than half of the questioned juveniles had committed crimes in a state of intoxication.

The shortcomings of state agencies designed to struggle against juvenile delinquency create in juveniles the feeling of impunity of committing antisocial actions.

Among these shortcomings there should be mentioned the weakness of militia preventive work with juveniles. Sometimes effective measures are not taken to prevent juvenile crime and for the early discovery of offences committed by juveniles.

During the investigation of juvenile offences and the hearing of these cases in courts investigators' and judges' specialization are not always observed. This lessens the educational influence on juveniles before their arrival in colony.

In connection with the discussion, we would like to cite the description given by a juvenile (Bashkir ASSR colony) of his way to the crime: "My father had a previous conviction for ruffianly behavior. He frequently organized drinking parties at home. He did not look after me and he didn't care what I was doing and where I was being. I made friends with a group of boys most of them were working at that time. We frequently drank vodka paying with money earned by them. Sometimes these boys lended money to me and the others. In order to pay that money back I in a group of adolescents started at nights to tear fur-caps off passers-by, then we stole cigarettes from the shop counter. After that we committed a theft in an apartment by removing a window frame, but we were arrested."

The struggle against juveniles' delinquency (as with criminality in general) is conducted by two groups of social prevention measures: general and special ones.

The Constitution of the USSR and constitutions of the union republics are the state and legal bases for all measures of social prevention of criminality. The Constitution of the USSR, for example, guarantees the realization of a series of the general measures of social prevention and, among them, free education and professional training for youth (Article 25.45); the possibility of moral and aesthetical education, the growth of the cultural level (Article 27); the right to work (Article 40); the right to rest and leisure (Article 41). It takes the family into protection of the state (Article 53). All these and other provisions of the Constitution of the USSR guarantee the rights, freedoms, and legal interests of citizens and by this creates in the rising generation a confidence in its future and the possibility to display its individuality in its work for the benefit of our society.

Among others promoting the realization of the general measures for the prevention of juvenile delinquency there should be mentioned the principles of civil legislation of the USSR and union republics and civil codes of union republics which guarantee, for example, the right of succession for juveniles. The principles of legislation of the USSR and union republics of matrimony and family and corresponding codes of union republics form the legal base for providing education and establish the responsibilities of parents towards their children. These and some other laws are not directed immediately to the prevention of juvenile delinquency, but it is difficult to overestimate their significance for this work.

On the whole, general measures of crime prevention are realized in the process of building communism in our country. In the CPSU Programme it is pointed out that: "The growth of well-being, of cultural level and the consciousness of the working masses creates all the conditions for the eradication of criminality. The Communist Party and the Soviet Government conduct considerable work in this direction. There is constant growing of material well-being and level of culture and education of the population. The salary of workers and employees is increasing, the rate of old age pensions is rising, the pensional provision for collective farmers is established, universal ten-year education of children has become compulsory for all, etc."

The struggle against juvenile delinquency is carried out in the process of the administration of justice as well. The democratic principles of the judicial system are laid down in the Constitution of the USSR; independence of judges is guaranteed as well as their subordination only to the law (Article 155); equality of citizens is assured before the law and justice (Article 156); the accused are ensured the right of defence (Article 158) among other rights.

The special measures taken for the prevention of juvenile crimes and other offences first of all are directed towards eliminating inadequate family education, shortcomings in school education, overcoming the lack of employment opportunity, and education of juveniles at work; organization of leisure time for teenagers; placement and assistance to juveniles who live in unfavorable life and education conditions; and improvement of the efficiency of the legal organs.

The peculiarity of the special measures, as they apply to the juveniles, consists in the fact that they may be directed not only at offenders but under certain circumstances on to their parents.

The social approach to the prevention of juvenile delinquency is subdivided into educational measures and educational compulsory measures. To educational measures we may attribute labor, ideological-political and moral and legal education. As an example, we may cite the legal education for both the juveniles and their parents. It includes not only acquaintance with law, but also training to obey the law, and encourages juveniles to accept legal rules as imperative norms of behavior. The principles of soviet law are taught in all secondary modern schools, in specialized technical schools, and junior technical colleges; there are also people's universities that provide legal knowledge to youth and parents. The legal education also is disseminated by radio and television in special programs such as "Man and Law," the mass magazine "Man and Law," and in *Knowledge*.

All the work connected with the legal education of population is headed by Coordinating Council functioning under the Ministry of Justice of the USSR; this Council includes representatives of various ministries and public organization.

Among the educational-compulsory measures there may be cited, for example, fining of parents or juvenile having his own earnings for an offence committed by him.

Presently, in the USSR, in order to put into practice the special measures both of educational and compulsory character, there is a system of state public organizations which are specially responsible for conducting the work aimed at the prevention of juvenile offences. In the districts, towns and regions, or in republic the preventive work with juveniles is organized by boards of juvenile affairs. These are state institutions composed of deputies of the Soviets, representatives of the trade-union, Komsomol, and other public organizations. The employees of institu-

136

tions which, by the character of their work, are entrusted with the duty of preventing juvenile delinquency also are members. The Boards provide inspectors to work with children.

The main tasks of the boards of juvenile affairs consist in the prevention of neglect of children and of juvenile offences, the employment of juveniles, and protection of their rights. The boards coordinate the efforts of state agencies and public organizations, examine cases of juvenile offences and control the detention facilities. They organize education for the juveniles through the Ministry of Internal Affairs and other special institutions.

The Commissions, as an alternative to punishment, can impose educative measures on the adolescent only only if he committed a minor crime (serious crimes are handled by the courts), but also if he committed any other antisocial acts. Commissions also can impose measures on the parents of the delinquent adolescents, including public reprimand or fines of 30 rubles. They can refer the case of parents to the comrades' court, or also they can apply to the people's court to deprive the parents of their parental rights.

Along with the commissions there are inspection boards and reception and disposition centers for juveniles. These institutions are administered by the Ministry of Internal affairs. There are specialized schools for children and adolescents who need special conditions of education and specialized vocational schools. These schools are operated under the control of local Soviets' of people's deputies and their executive committees, commissions for cases of minors. These specialized state institutions function in cooperation with young communist league and trade-union organizations, sport, cultural, and educational organizations, public order squads, and with other state and public organizations.

Inspection boards, under the Ministry of Internal Affairs, are of great importance in the prevention of juvenile delinquency. Their work is devoted to all types of juvenile delinquents: those discharged from colonies, those given suspended sentences, or those assigned to educational programs as an alternative to criminal punishment as well as to those who have been released from specialized corrective institutions, to those who committed offences, involving measures of social or administrative ascendency, habitual drinkers. They also deal with parents who neglect their parental duties and with those who incite juveniles to commit antisocial acts.

Juvenile reception and disposition centers have as their main objective to render humane assistance to those juvenile delinquents who for some reason are in need of it. These centers temporarily give shelter to children and adolescents of the age from three to 18, attend to their future life, either getting them a home or placing them in an educational institution. Juveniles may be kept in these centers for the time needed to arrange their immediate future but for no longer than 30 days.

To help the centers in their educational activities, factories, cultural and educational institutions, and public organizations give them their voluntary assistance.

Specialized schools for children and adolescents in need of special conditions of education and specialized vocational training have been established and instruction to understand and respect soviet law.

The educational process in specialized schools and specialized vocational schools is characterized by a strict policy, an efficient daily routine, constant supervision. All these factors promote productive work, other socially useful activities and a well-spent leisure time.

Juvenile delinquents aged from 11 to 14 are referred to specialized schools on the grounds of the decision made by the commissions for the cases of juveniles of the city or district (local) Soviets of people's deputies' executive committees. Juvenile delinquents aged from 14 to 18 are sent to specialized vocational schools either in accordance with the decisions of the commissions for the cases of juveniles of the executive committees of local or city Soviets of people's deputies, or in accordance with the ruling of the court. Juveniles are kept in specialized educational-corrective institutions until they are reeducated, but for no more than three years.

Criminal legal proceedings for the cases of juveniles are regulated by special norms of criminal procedure law, in the RSFSR Code of Criminal Procedure. There is a whole chapter devoted to this matter (Article 391–402). Legal proceedings are somewhat different in the cases of juvenile offenders. And we can trace these differences in the procedure from the very moment the information on the case of juvenile offence arrives. If the juvenile offender is under the age of criminal liability (the age of criminal liability is 14 for grave crimes and 16 for other crimes) legal proceedings cannot be instituted against him. The same applies if it is possible to impose on him measures of social ascendancy.

But if the case is brought before the court it is investigated only by the investigator assigned by the agencies which deal with the cases of juveniles. While conducting preliminary investigation and examination in court, the investigator and the judge should pay particular attention to determining the age of the juvenile, his life style, his education and the causes, and conditions that lead to the offence (for example, whether or not there were adult inciters or other accomplices). If the juvenile is known to be mentally retarded but not mentally ill, it should be established whether he was fully aware of the significance of his actions.

Irrespective of the fact that the child has legal representation in court, the defendant is also provided with a counselor for the defense during the process of preliminary investigation.

Together with the counselor for the defense, a social educator is also present both at the interrogations during preliminary investigation and in court.

While trying a case in court it is absolutely obligatory to discuss the possibility of imposing on the offender educative measures rather than criminal punishment. They could include imposing on the defendant the duty of publicly or in some other form apologizing to the victim; imposing on the offender an official, severe reprimand; placing of the offender under strict supervision of his parents or guardians; imposing caution; sending of the juvenile to a specialized educational-corrective institution. Or, the defendant may be given a sentence of a maximum three year prison term for the first time. However, the court may, considering the nature and seriousness of the committed crime, the personality of the accused and other circumstances of the case, respite the punsihment to a term ranging from six months to two years.

All the measures described above ensure the correction and re-education of juveniles without isolating them from the society, provided that they are placed under the control of state agencies, public organizations, and labor collectives. According to sample data, the number of the repeat offenders among the juveniles with suspended sentences does not exceed the rate of 1 to 3 percent.

The supervising functions of public procuracy in the field of juvenile delinquency prevention are aimed at detecting and punishing violations of the law and at protecting children's rights. Public prosecutors see that the law is strictly observed during the investigation and in court when the cases of juveniles are being tried. The procuracy coordinates the activities of law enforcement bodies including their activities in the field of juvenile crime prevention.

Public agencies operating at the places of work and residence of the juveniles play an active role in juvenile crime prevention. At the places where juveniles work and live the public agencies are the collectives of workers and their organizations such as volunteer public order squads, comrades' courts, and councils of prevention. Volunteer public order squads are formed from the members of the collectives of workers. Their main task is maintaining public order. But they also take part in juvenile crime prevention activities. They talk to juvenile offenders and their parents, and appoint instructors and sponsors for those juveniles who were given respite or for those with suspended sentences.

Comrades' courts are still another form of public participation to combat crime. They are formed out of distinguished members of working collectives. They try cases of minor offences such as a breach of the peace and cases of misconduct, which pose no grave danger to the society. As for juveniles cases they deal with the acts of negligence of parental duties. The councils also deal with juvenile misconduct in the place of work. Offenders may be deprived of some privileges stipulated by collective labor contract. Comrades' court may pass censure on the offender, bind the offender to apologise, make up for wrong-doing or impose a fine. Councils of prevention also play a most important role in juvenile crime prevention.

The councils are elected at the general meeting of workers and are progressive workers, members of the Communist party, trade-union, and Komsomol organizations.

The volunteer public order squads and comrades' courts are set up also at places of residence, especially the centers of educational and preventive activities. They operate from house manager's office in close cooperation with house management committees and other public organizations.

The preventive measures taken in accordance with the plans described above, promote the detection of juveniles and families in need of supervision. They are used to determine those bodies and organizations which can deal with delinquency effectively and improve of state agencies and public organizations that function in the field of juvenile crime prevention.

8

Switzerland

H. Veillard-Cybulska

This chapter was written by Mrs. Henryka Veillard-Cybulska of Lausanne, Switzerland. For 16 years she served as a judge in the Juvenile court in Poland where she was also assistant professor of applied psychology at Lodz University. Her credentials include degrees in law, social science, psychology and criminology. While her contribution is a careful account of the social and juridical services for children throughout Switzerland it reflects her long experience as researcher, teacher, judge, and author. She sets her chapter in the middle of the international scene and provides a useful perspective. She has written widely in the field of child welfare and delinquency and currently is co-editor of the *International Child Welfare Review.* She is Deputy Secretary General of the International Association of Juvenile and Family Court Magistrates.

Editor

Switzerland is a federal state in which the sovereign power is divided between the confederation and the cantons. Some of the cantons have enjoyed independence for centuries, others for only a much shorter time. For these historical reasons, but also for economical, social, and political ones, there are considerable variations in both the administrative and judicial systems from one canton to another. The two laws which regulate child protection (the Swiss Civil Code in 1912 and the Swiss Penal Code in 1942), are standard but the organization, the procedure and the administration of justice and of social work are the responsibility of each canton, and the law as it is applied, is as varied as the cantons themselves.

Things being so in Switzerland, juvenile justice, as formulated in the title, cannot be explained here in all its scope. We have therefore decided to limit ourselves to the short survey of the social welfare—"social justice"—and the judicial protection of children in need of care and of juvenile offenders—"legal justice." In general social welfare is organized on democratic and federal lines. There are numerous private organizations, and many of these are subsidized by the cantons or federal agencies, which prescribe certain provisions and supervise their activities. The most important are Pro Juventute, Pro Familia, Pro Infirmis, and Pro Senectute, which are regional agencies working with volunteers.

These are public agencies, including the *Guardianship Authority* and the Youth Offices. Their structure and responsibilities will be described later.

JUDICIAL PROTECTION

Each canton has its own judicial organization for adults as well as for juveniles. There are two systems for juveniles; the ordinary court with a specialized youth prosecutor, and the special juvenile court in French- (except for Neuchatel) and Italian-speaking cantons. A few cantons of German-speaking Switzerland, such as Basel, St. Gallen, Bern, also have the special jurisdictions for juveniles. The other German cantons rely upon the school authority of the commune as the judicial body for children. The Basel and Neuchatel Cantons have a tutelary (or family) and juvenile courts.

144

The ordinary courts are supervised by the "Jugendanwalt" and the special courts by a president who often collaborates with the Youth Protection Office.

Except in Neuchatel and Basel, the juvenile courts are exclusively penal tribunals. "Care and protection" and "Beyond control" and other cases are dealt with by a special body an administrative body of the commune, which is a kind of local court in French speaking Switzerland.*

We shall describe their competences and work more in detail later.

SOCIAL, ADMINISTRATIVE, AND LEGAL ORGANIZATION OF CHILD WELFARE

As was previously said, in Switzerland, child care and assistance of children are administered by various associations and institutions. However, when the physical, psychic, or moral development of the child is seriously threatened, the Guardianship Authority intervenes, and is assisted by Child Protection Committees.

The principal aim of the Guardianship Authority is to protect children if their parents are dead, unknown, untraceable, or have had their parental rights limited or withdrawn. Much attention is also paid to protect the interests of the child born, or to be born, out of wedlock. The Swiss Civil Code stipulates that the Guardianship Authorities shall appoint a trustee for the child born out of wedlock as soon as they are informed of the birth or as soon as the future mother informs them of her pregnancy. This trustee is required to discover the father, to obtain the recognition of the latter or his pledge to accept the legal obligations (including payment of maternity costs and a maintenance allow-

---

* Cf. Protection penale des mineur en Suisse (in French only) par Henryka Veillard-Cybulska Tiré à part de "L'ENFANT," Recueils de la Société Jean Bodin, T. 38, 1977, p.111–180.

ance) in default of which he, as guardian, must institute a paternity suit. Since this is a delicate mission, it is often entrusted to a lawyer appointed as trustee or to a statutory guardian. The code also requires that when a divorced father or mother remarries, and when circumstances require, a guardian must be appointed to safeguard the interests of the child of the first marriage in the second marriage.

Because there is a shortage of private guardians, special agencies carry out the guardianship role in some cantons. This service was first and foremost concerned with administrative aspects of the task. Gradually, attempts were made to render the guardian/ ward relations more human. There was greater contact with social workers, parents and minors themselves, who became subjects rather than the objects of guardianship.

The services, working now with a view to prevention, collaborate with the specialists (psychologists, psychiatrists, educators, and social workers) with the child guidance clinics, and other specialized centers. These also began to play a more important role. A guardian can always obtain help and advice from those services. In some cases, such a service in practice may take almost total responsibility for the child in trouble, whilst the guardian remains his legal representative.

The work with children in trouble and with their families and measures to be taken, whether they are socially, administratively, or legally based, use varied assistance, welfare, education, rehabilitation and care methods. The choice of the appropriate measures is usually preceded by inquiries and recommendations by social workers or other specialists. The police also provide information if need be.

The measures to be taken by the competent authority, when the health, safety, morality or education of a child is threatened, can be divided into three main categories of severity.

The first of these is the *warning* or *admonition* either purely and simply or with on-going support from a social worker who gives assistance, advice, guidance, and friendship. The second involves the temporary separation of the child from his parents. The child may be placed in the care of a "trustworthy person" (generally a close relative, family friend, apprenticeship master, among others) or a foster family selected, supported and supervised by the competent authorities. They represent the parents and have the right to be heard before any decision is taken with regard to children entrusted to them. The child may be also sent to a small family-type-home or placed in a specialized institution where appropriate treatement and care can be given. In all these cases the child remains in contact with his father and mother.

The third measure involves the *withdrawal of parental rights;* ties between the child and one or both of his parents are severed. This requires a care of *Guardianship order* (if both parents are concerned) and/or removal from the family home. The type of *residential care* is dependent on the need of the child. The withdrawal of parental rights and the removal from the family home should be *exceptional.*

Foster care, more to be recommended that residential care from a psychological and socioeducational standpoint, has proved to be very difficult to administer.[1] A number of problems face the authorities concerned: the recruitment and selection of foster parents, their psychological and educational training, the moral and financial support granted to them, and also the means of continuous supervision both discreet and effective. Thus, social workers or other competent persons visit them, and when necessary provide support in the upbringing process. Meetings, courses, and conferences are organized and information is circulated. But there are cases of conflict and changes of foster home, both being negative for the child involved. A new law on filiation is more favorable to the foster parents. They have recently created an association to better defend their rights.

1. See Cartee Romand, ed. "Fiches sociales" (Lausanne) and "Introduction au Travail Social et à L'Action Sociale," Cartel à Romand, ed.

The placement in an institution as a protective or educational measure is the most serious step to take, and the most difficult to accomplish successfully. The placement can be the best or the worst solution; it can sometimes be more harmful than the situation from which the child was removed. Although priority must be given to the treatment of the child in the family, it might become necessary to separate the child from his family. Treatment should be focussed on efforts to rehabilitate the child with a view to returning him to his family. Too often, however, these principles are insufficiently put into practice. In Switzerland, as in many other countries, institutional care is in crisis. The establishments are half-empty, and some have been closed.

The socioeducational work of the official agencies done on a legal basis, is supplemented by many private institutions and associations. The most important among them is Pro Juventute. This private welfare foundation, founded in 1912, gets its financial resources from the sale of special postage stamps and greeting cards. Pro Juventute works with all age groups of children up to 20 years old. The leading organizations concerned with social welfare are linked together in the Swiss National Conference on Social Welfare—Swiss National Committee of the International Council on Social Welfare.

Social work for small children is provided in numerous day-nurseries homes for mothers (mainly unmarried) and babies, special children's homes, and kindergarten. Various private and public institutions provide help for nursing mothers and their babies through personal advice, babysitting, visiting nurses, gifts of baby linen and perambulators, as well as the organization of householdhelps, and so on.

Welfare work for school children is mainly organized by the communal authorities for the private associations. They distribute food to some schools in mountain areas and to day centers. They also administer the school medical service to control hygienic conditions and to provide the health and dental care for both pupils and teachers. They operate holiday and recuperation facilities for school children including camps. Educational centers are established in larger towns for evening courses and discussion-and-study groups for parent-teacher associations, as well as galleries for art exhibitions and libraries.

The associations also aid adolescents and young people who leave school. First of all they provide them with a *professional orientation* and/or a professional training or suitable job. Vocational guidance, is provided free of charge. Every canton has a central office for vocational guidance, and the vocational advisers are employed by local authorities. Their task is becoming more and more difficult considered the increasing number of professions and specializations, the instability of youths working in spite of the unemployment, the attitude contesting the modern conditions of the work, and so on. Therefore, the Swiss Civil Code requires parents to take the aptitudes and wishes of their children into account as much as possible. If the parents are unable to pay for professional training, grants are available from communal, cantonal or federal funds.

An *apprenticeship* is usually served in industry or a trade. The training and exams are regulated by a federal law and supervised by special cantonal offices. Vocational guidance is provided by the Swiss Association for Vocational Guidance assisted by the federal authorities. *Youth organizations* are also involved. They organize lectures, courses, and discussions preparatory to professional, social, and familial life. The national youth associations are linked together in the Swiss Federation of Youth Associations. Recreation also is provided for, primarily consisting of the meeting of young people to help them to shape their personalities. Lecture centers for young people are mostly in larger towns but also in larger communes. They have playgrounds, rooms for hobbies, libraries, and swimmingpools.

PROTECTION OF MENTALLY AND PHYSICALLY HANDICAPPED CHILDREN

In 1960, *National Invalididty Insurance* was established not only to provide financial help for handicapped children, but also to offer reeducation and rehabilitation. Two executive agencies manage these services: *cantonal commissions* and *regional offices.* The cantonal authorities are responsible for special schools. The regional offices organise the special professional training and work for the adolescents and also provide workshops. They are aided by many private institutions and organizations such as Pro Infirmis, the Swiss Federation for the Integration of the Handicapped, and the Swiss Union of the Seminaries of Curative Pedagogy. Pro Infirmis is the most important private association, it collaborates closely with the official agencies. Centers for part-time jobs are organized by the Swiss Association for the Integrated of Handicapped.

A wide range of institutions, both public and private are devoted to assisting families. In all cantons, family allowances are paid, by law, at a certain income level. On a federal basis, special allowances and other forms of economic and social aid to families in need are also foreseen. Besides the organized help offered by the official agencies, the family protection movement is led by the federal association, Pro Familia, to which various organizations are affiliated. Pro Familia is a member of the International Union of Family Organizations, founded in 1947 and presided over by Swiss Juvenile Court Judge.

Those providing the legal family aid are often confronted with the arduous task of interpreting and applying the law. For instance, Art. 283 of the Swiss Civil Code states that the guardianship authorities take the necessary steps to ensure the welfare of the child when the father and/or mother "do not fulfil their duties." Such a disposition, which prejudges the parents behavior as blameworthy, often made cooperation with the latter very difficult. If a supervision order was made, for instance, the social worker might encounter considerable trouble in establishing a relationship based on confidence. The "educational assistance" was in practice reduced to a short "check-up" visit, devoid of any supportive content and only limited to a superficial conversation to safeguard relations. Conflict may arise between agencies. Cases are recorded when neither the divorce judge nor the guardianship authority was willing to deal with a request concerning the welfare of a child; other social services, in the meantime, could not intervene on the child's behalf. Nevertheless, judicial intervention should be applied continuously by specialized judges. Although no legal or social organs could resolve all the problems created by family breakdowns, a step forward should be made by putting some order in the labyrinth of competences and organizing a formation in human sciences for the juvenile and family court magistrates.

In 1973, an international conference of experts on youth assistance, held in Bern, was primarily aimed at strengthening the legal position of children and adolescents. Recommendations were made regarding a number of appropriate *modifications in family law.* A commission would deal with the overall coordination of the law's application. The youth advisory office should organize an annual conference on assistance to youth where ideas could be exchanged and recommendations sent to the competent bodies and authorities, so a plan of action can be drawn up to meet the needs of the moment. Then, in 1978, some important modifications were made to the law changing the status of children and parent-child relations. Parents' authority must now be understood as a socioeducational function, jointly exercised by both the father and the mother for the benefit of the child and no longer as simply a series of parental prerogatives. Both father and mother are to exercise the parental authority.

In case of a conflict, the parents and the child should collaborate in order to find a way of solving the problem. As in the juvenile penal law, emphasis has been placed on the interests of the child rather than on those of adult society, as was the case in the past. In the event of conflict of these interests, those concerning the child must take priority. Education must consist in progressively developing the self-reliance and the sense of responsibility of children and in preparing them for adult roles in a changing society.

In order to stress this new approach of family education the law declares that parents must on the one hand, allow children freedom to organize their lives in accordance with degree of maturity, and, on the other, insofar as possible, take into account the opinions of children concerning important affairs.

Official protective measures are so similar to those inscribed in juvenile penal law that it may be asked whether it would not be appropriate to combine them in a unified juvenile civil and penal law.[2] This might be desirable in view of the fact that the law would oblige cantons to coordinate the activities of all child welfare agencies, including notably those maintaining liaison between juvenile penal law services and guardianship authorities, which now often do not cooperate with each other.

LEGAL PROTECTION AND TREATMENT OF JUVENILE OFFENDERS

Before speaking of legal action concerning juvenile offenders, it should be most useful to know the extent of juvenile delinquency in Switzerland as reflected in the federal statistics. Alas, we have no data relating to minors under 15 years of age and the penal record of adolescents (between 15 and 18 years) contains only the most serious crimes. So, statistical figures hide more than they reveal. The data of cantonal reports cannot be summarized because their methods of defining juvenile offences differ from one canton to the other.[3] Our knowledge and experience

------

2. See H. Veillard-Cybulska. *Judicial Protection of the Youth All Over the World* (Brussels: Association of Juvenile Court Magistrates, 1974), p. 85ff.

3. See H. Veillard-Cybulska. *Aspects of Juvenile Delinquency in Switzerland* (The Swiss Society of Penal Minors Law). (in French only), Roneo, 63p. 10 diagrams and tables.

teach us, nevertheless, that juvenile delinquency in Switzerland is as prevalent as that is the Western European countries. Over 65 percent of the offences are against property (such as stealing or shoplifting) and they have increased from year to year. Offences concerning traffic violations and drugs have risen in recent years and so have the offences committed by girls and children. Delinquency is highest in the urban areas, where drug addiction and traffic offences are also increasing. Offences of violence have been rather rare in Switzerland in comparison to other Western countries, and so have been acts of terrorism attributed to youth. Murders are rare.

Generally speaking, over 75 percent of juvenile offenders are occasional and their delinquency may be imputed to juvenile turbulence, indiscipline, immaturity, and so on. The fact, however, that the proportion of the young recidivists does not change, remaining between 20 and 30 percent is very disquieting. It demands a further reform in the treatment of the most serious cases.

The treatment of juvenile offenders is dealt with according to the Swiss Penal Code, for Switzerland has no special law for children and adolescent delinquents. The code distinguishes four groups of young people: children under seven, who are not responsible before the penal law, children between the ages of seven and 15, adolescents between 15 and 18, and young adults between 18 and 25. Children and adolescents, however, are not dealt the penalties given to adults but are subjected to educative and reeducative measures or disciplinary punishments. Young adults are treated by the ordinary court, but the latter is advised to mitigate the punishment.

Educational measures for juveniles consist in admonition, educative assistance (probation), placement in foster families or a foster home, or placement in an institution (educative or reeducative). Juvenile punishment ranges from reprimands, fines (for adolescents only), to placement in a detention attendance center. If the measures applied have achieved the desired goal, they are

153

discontinued. The most important aspect of the new reform is that the individual treatment of all junveniles is possible, even if they are placed in a fairly strict environment. For a more effective application of the measures and sanctions, the Federal Council has the power to authorize other penalties that are not specified in the code (Art. 397bis SPC) for a limited period.

PROCEDURE

A special characteristic of Swiss legislation is that the procedural dispositions concerning minors precede the substantive law. The judge has each case investigated before the trial. He has to gather information concerning behavior, education, family, and the social situation of the young delinquent, and, if necessary, to get expert opinion on his physical or mental health, and, in the case of young adults, their ability to work and on their work training.

In Switzerland, the police refer to juvenile jurisdiction all children and adolescents who have broken the penal or special law. (However, in collaboration with juvenile court magistrates, Minors' Brigades, Police Social Workers, and women police have come to emphasize preventive measures.) The court hearing for minors consists of an inquiry concerning the facts (one speaks of facts, not of offences), investigation concerning *the personality* (a psycho-medical assessment if necessary) and *social conditions* (family life, and friends, for instance). The hearing of a juvenile case is usually held privately, with a lawyer to help the juvenile. *The disposition* of the case should be in accordance with the spirit of the welfare of minor. Further, he himself, his parents, or his lawyer may always appeal to a higher court. The more important punishments or measures ordered with regard to adolescents (not children) are entered in the judicial record. They are erased when the juvenile reaches the age of 20. In any case all juvenile treatment ceases to have effect at the age of 20 or 22 for adolescents.

It is from this point of view that we shall try to describe some experiences and characteristic treatment of juvenile offenders in Switzerland. As one example the Bernese Oberland Court has conducted an experiment for providing group therapy, in a natural setting. A group involved in this experiment comprised eight juvenile delinquents and two social workers (a man and a woman) who led the discussion. The 21 weekly meetings took place in the evenings and were held over a period of about six months. Each meeting was devoted to the discussion of the problems of the juveniles in attendance, punctuated with some recreation and sports activities. The participants discuss the "causes" of their delinquency: being led astray, rivalry, impulsive behavior, jealousy, inferiority complexes, the desire to be admired, conflicts with parents, teachers and the police, relations with girls, and sexual problems. Thereafter, discussions centered on the consequences of "legal conviction", the rules and regulations of community life, loyalty, honesty, and regard for the interests of others. Initially, the youths had difficulty in concentrating on the discussion themes and they tried to distract attention from serious debate with idle conversation and games. But finally they agreed to talk about their problems. At the end, the participants stated their great appreciation for having being given this opportunity to discuss freely with adults who had shown patience, comprehension, and interest in them and who took what they had to say seriously. Judging by their remarks, the youths gained a new image of the "establishment," and for their part the two wocial workers learned a great deal from these young people.

As another example, the judge may oblige the juvenile to perform some work task. Yet, such a measure should not be resented as a punishment but regarded as voluntary action by means of which the minor attempts to rehabilitate himself. It may be a reparation for damage cause, or work for the community (in the municipal gardens, or for the Red Cross) or for disabled and sick persons (one or more half-days in a hospital), for the aged or children (in a children's home), or as a preventive measure. The judge can send juveniles who break traffic regulations to a course given by the police. Those who inadvertently cause a fire may be sent to collaborate with a club of "fire-watchers" or to assist firemen. Young vandals are employed to clean beaches, lake sides, public places and parks.

The Swiss Association of Juvenile Penal Law discussed at its annual meeting the application of such measures as an official sanction, evaluated the results achieved, and felt that they had been encouraging. In order that the measure be effective, it must be accepted both by the minor and his parents. Re-education through work also has been imposed on young adults. The new dispositions formulating this type of treatment state that if the offence is due to a gravely disturbed character development or if there is a danger that, left to himself, the young man lead a life of misconduct, the judge may, instead of punishment, send him to an institution where he is reeducated by work, especially if this measure can prevent further crimes or offences.

It is the intention of the penal code to make work training a really educational means providing proper apprenticeship, which can be undertaken outside an institution. Most of the chapter dealing with young adults is dedicated to the description of this treatment-by-work concept. The institutions for work training must differ from other institutions. All inmates should be given work suited to their abilities, work that will enable them to earn their living after discharge. Character improvement, the development of intellectual and physical maturity, and the professional training should also be encouraged. If these hopeful guidelines are really put into practice, results are likely to be more satisfactory.

As another example, of so-called special treatment is now provided. It serves therapeutic and preventive purposes. It may be ordered to help subnormal minors, mentally defectives, the infirm, alcoholics, drug addicts, and individuals whose emotional or moral development is disturbed or retarded. Thus the judge

156

can provide the treatment the young delinquent needs, but which he has not received before. It is, however, left to the specialist to decide what is the best treatment. But the special treatment is not limited to medical or psychological methods. It is often combined with other educational measures.

As the minors develop, *new measures may take place of the previous ones* at any time, even if the minor has committed no new offence. The possibility to modify the measures and their indeterminate duration are typical for the Swiss system. The judge must follow the evolution of the young and his needs. Since the special treatment does not imply a moral condemnation or disapproval of the minor or of his parents, it is more easily accepted. For example, one of the girl offenders nicknamed "Squint-eyed" has been a shoplifter. Her commital to the care of a "trustworthy person" (her aunt) under supervision of a probation officer seemed to be the best measure. But the girl was arrogant with her tutors who tried to improve her bad conduct and she continued to steal. Then, the special treatment was applied including psychotherapy. The psychologist devoted much time to this treatment. Finally, the young girl was persuaded by the therapist and the judge to undergo an eye operation. After, she was not only physically but also mentally changed. She stopped stealing, found a boy firend, got married, and there was no further trouble with her. She is now the mother of three children and a good wife. As another example, a 16-year-old boy stole different motor vehicles for his own and his friends use or to break up into pieces and sell the parts. Eventually he has been placed in an institution for wayward adolescents but he was successful neither in the school nor in professional training. Twice he made suicidal attempts and escaped from the hospital in a stolen medical car. So the special treatment was applied by the psychiatric help. The doctor succeeded in detaching him from his bad habit and to undertake an apprenticeship in mechanical training. After he had passed his examinations, the family helped him to buy a car. He began to work in a garage and continued voluntarily with the therapeutical treatment as aftercare.

Educational assistance—previously called "surveilled (controlled) liberty" has been imposed most often by the juvenile courts as by the guardianship authorities for troubled children and parents in trouble. This method of treatment allows the child to remain within his family-circle. In cases where educational assistance has been chosen, the application of this measure is entrusted to a professional social worker or to a specialised educator or again to a probation officer for juvenile delinquents. Unfortunately, there are generally too few of these professionals, and they often must work with dozens of minors. As a result, the educative value of this measure is very reduced. Various actions have been proposed to overcome this problem. First of all, the judge must be informed about the nature of the educational assistance and its possibilities and advantages. Before pronouncing measures to be taken, the judge must prepare the ground for their execution and encourage collaboration. When the disturbed behavior of the minor results from lack of parental education, the judge should never be satisfied with concentrating solely on the young girl or boy. Intervention of the guardianship authorities often becomes necessary. This intervention may sometimes go as far as to restrict parental rights and may even lead to the withdrawal of parental authority, but it is exceptional. If parents seem capable of providing a minimum of collaboration, everything must be done to encourage and associate them with the efforts of the social worker. In cases of conflict between the social worker and parents, the two parties can be summoned to court to explain their points of view and, in order to try and reach a solution. If however, differences of opinion persist, only the judge can intervene as a mediator to try to settle the dispute, for example, by convincing the parents to forego their prerogatives for a certain period of time. If the judge reaches the conclusion that the difficulties are due to the personality of the social worker, he can propose that the task be transferred to someone else. However, such transfers are delicate both in relation to the "assisted" and the "assistant," and should only be ordered with great caution.

The judge also may impose rules of conduct, either positive rules, such as those requiring the minor to attend school, go to work, take courses, repair damages, or negative; excluding the minor from associating with certain persons or groups, residing in a particular place, consuming alcoholic beverages or smoking, and taking drugs. The judge can also appoint two social workers, one for the parents, to help them or to overcome their neutral opposition, and the other devoting himself exclusively to the minor. This solution may lead, however, to a conflict between the two social workers, which can only be avoided inasmuch as both workers act in perfect harmony. This requires good self-control and above-average emotional maturity. Finally, the judge may impose fines or detention (14 days maximum). This is provided for under Swiss code. Both sanctions may be ordered with benefit of reprieve and probation. This probatory period can last six months, minimum, to three years, maximum. It can constitute a useful deterrent in cases where the minor infringes the rules of conduct. Finally, the judge can place the minor in an institution, which is the most serious step, if the minor continues to show clear signs of delinquency or to present severe behavioral difficulties. The judge has a choice between a number of different kinds of institutions including children and adolescent educational homes, homes for minors with some freedom, houses for re-education, and homes that provide therapy.

If the minor is institutionalized, but with some freedom, he will be cared for from morning until evening and provided suitable school or professional training. Special educators are in charge of these minors who enjoy also further attention from doctors and psychologists. Social workers serve as a link between the institution and the family where the child or adolescent spends the night, weekends, and holidays.

If the minor is sent to a reeducational home, he is confined during mealtime, free time, and at night. They attend school or continue professional training or work during the day.

Because of the epidemic of drug addiction in the last few years, special centers for users of narcotics have been set up. These include free clinics and homes where addicts may "drop-in" on their own initiative. According to new conceptions, the social workers consider that they are no longer the agent of the "system" willing only to transmit, or even to impose, the social values which are contested nowadays. They will be the creators of a new social pedagogy, and become the catalysts of the interests of the youth.

Therapy centers have been created recently for the most difficult minors by the Federal Division of Justice has elaborated the "Directives" concerning the treatment of *particularly difficult adolescents.* Such minors include those whom existing establishments refuse to take in owing to the gravity of the case; or because their disturbances impede the application of educational measures, or because they display an "intolerable behavior." The minor must be a minimum of 15 years old, and can be held until he is 25. He must have been held previously in an establishment provided for under the penal law, and be suffering from serious personality problems which cannot be treated satisfactorily in these other homes, but are likely to react favorably to treatment. This treatment must be of the highest quality. The directives stipulate that the director of the therapy center must be either a qualified psychiatrist or psychologist who has considerable aptitude test experience (200 hours at the minimum), and the educational and therapeutic staff must equal the numbers of boarders. It must guarantee the possibility for boarders to complete an apprenticeship or to exercise a profession outside the institution.

The therapy center can be associated with an educational home but should be isolated. These special institutions must undertake systematic and scientific evaluations of the effectiveness of their activities. The results of the evaluative studies must always be placed at the disposal of the Federal Justice Division.

Aftercare is a new program that is carried out by the offices for protection of youth and by the Patronage societies. The way a young delinquent is treated after his release may determine whether becomes a recidivist or not, and many juvenile court magistrates believe, rightly too, that is is just as important as care itself. Thus, the president of the Juvenile Court in Lausanne tried to apply them with the help of specialists of human sciences and of some voluntary social-minded workers, ready to take an interest in and guide the young people after their release. The latter were encouraged to seek help for their problems not only from the social assistants but also from the judge. Some of them were even asked to befriend other pupils being assisted by social workers. By using this approach the boys and girls learn to understand others and themselves too, and to develop social maturity and responsibility. We should like to consider them not just as our "clients" but as our collaborators in the attempts to save the youth in danger of relapsing.

My own experiment in this field, made in Poland in the fifties, was influenced by the concept of the group therapy and psychodrama as well as by the Russian pedagogue Makarenko. We provided selected parolees with a challenge to their social mindedness. They made up a play in which they acted the roles of the juvenile delinquents, parents, judge, state attorney, barrister, probation officer. Thus experiencing again their own situation, they became aware of their own reactions and motives. This helped them to clarify their attitude toward the offence and society.[4]

With our Swiss juvenile offenders we did not go so far, but after we had worked for nearly two years with a group of seven adolescents and their parents, we selected two of them, whom we considered most suited, to act as voluntary social workers. They were prepared for one year by working with social assist-

4. H. Veillard-Cybulska, "An Aftercare Experiment in Poland," *International Journal of Offender Therapy,* Vol. II, No. 2 (1967), p. 63-67 .

ants. Treating them as responsible persons, not just as supervised parolees, taught them to become more independent and to make decisions for themselves and for the others. When they came up against difficulties with the others they could always discuss the case with us. We were never deceived nor disappointed by our two young collaborators.

Sometimes, though fortunately not too often, aftercare turns into permanent care for certain immature young who are quite unable to stand on their own feet. You have to watch over them, treat them, guide them discreetly so that this "fostering" does not prove too irritating or humiliating, and it may be necessary even to take an interest in their families and their comrades.

FINAL REMARKS

We have seen that Switzerland is a real mosaic of all possible regulations. This makes it difficult to understand the Swiss social and judicial system well, it has the advantage of being rich in multiple legal and social resources. As a positive result, troubled children and juvenile offenders are more and more considered as subjects of the law and no longer as objects to be manipulated for "their own good;" priority is given to treatment of the child *in* the family and not the child *and* the family. The first step is to help the parents and to establish a cooperative relationship with them through the social services and guidance clinics without resorting to coercive measures. It is less and less question of punishing them for the past, and more and more question of preparing them for the future; if it becomes necessary to place the child outside his family, treatment is provided to reunite them as quickly as possible. If this cannot be done, efforts are made to create an environment for the child similar to that of the family because it is considered more desirable to place the minor in small children's homes with house-parents rather that in institutions. The facilities and methods used in assistance, care, protection, re-education, rehabilitation—whether legal or social—have been more and more diversified and differentiated. This constitutes a real wealth of treatment of juvenile offenders if one compares these with the poverty and imperfection of means available to the adult-court. Human sciences and humanitarian ideas have brought about changes in the juvenile justice repression has given way to re-education and rejection has been replaced by rehabilitation.

The above statements lead us to look also at what *is negative* about the system of juvenile justice. In spite of good laws and the variety of measures to be taken, it often happens that the results may be dissapointing. The children and even parents feel guilt-ridden, embarrassed, irresolute, perplexed. The court appearance, and even the help of social services, can be a harrowing experience. This is often due to the fact that judges and other magistrates or members of official bodies are rarely specialists in child protection and have little or no background in human sciences. Their methods, especially with regard to a psycho-educational approach to anxious, difficult, and aggressive children or adolescents, often are inadequate or inappropriate. The division and overlapping of competence, and the formalities and slowness of procedure are also disconcerting for those who seek a rapid solution to their problems. The result is that the troubled child may find himself in trouble and in conflict not only with his parents but also with foster parents, guardians, trustees, social workers, and administrative officials. The legal texts and the social work were conceived to protect the young children; they are hardly now, if at all, adaptable to the actual situation of troubled adolescents, above all to those who question everything: family; school; marriage; and moral, social, and legal norms. For these reasons, the contradictions in the system should be, at least partially, resolved in the near future.

It would seem that the establishment of family courts may represent a potentially effective way of resolving a certain number of conflict situations in a constructive manner. Furthermore, new services must be set up for family guidance, and special counselling centers for the older adolescents, quite different from those that cater for children. The legal bases and the social orientation of the new forms of assistance to adolescents should focus on increasing their independence and responsibility.

Along with cooperation between child, family, and youth welfare agencies, cooperation from the community proves to be necessary. We must have an ever-growing number of individuals in society willing to collaborate with professional teams. The so-called "spontaneous" movement of youth, which manifests itself in mutual and community aid, wants more general and less professional social guidance. This shows the new social evolution. It is a tendency in a pluralistic society, which will be tolerant, liberal, egalitarian and human—and where hierarchic vertical structures will be substituted by more democratic and horizontal ones.

In the treatment of troubled children and juvenile delinquents and their parents, the science and justice—or rather science integrated in human justice—can find their natural field of operation. So far, only haphazard experiments have been carried out. It has not become an urgent necessity, that "committed" research must work towards concrete application: it must find its justification *in* and *through applications* and adhere to an orientation based on real needs. That is a new style in regards to methods of intervention must be adopted to constantly try to determine if a particular line of action is useful to the persons concerned. While participating in the treatment, the active research worker modifies his methods whenever necessary; at the same time he is able to evaluate the treatment.

The participation of the juvenile and family court magistrates is especially important. All the other specialists cannot have, in the same measure as the judge, an overall picture of the problems involved. He can visualize the entire scope of the problems, their change and evolution, as well as the practical solutions which should be translated into action. Such important functions cannot be carried out by ordinary magistrates, but by those who have specialized knowledge and a long experience and become totally "committed" to their work and research.

164

Index